D1030011

BOOKS AND HABITS

BOOKS AND HABITS

FROM THE LECTURES OF

LAFCADIO HEARN

Selected and Edited with an Introduction

by

JOHN ERSKINE

Professor of English
Columbia University

Essay Index Reprint Series

BOOKS FOR LIBRARIES PRESS

FREEPORT, NEW YORK

First Published 1921
Reprinted 1968

LIBRARY OF CONGRESS CATALOG CARD NUMBER:
68-20308

PRINTED IN THE UNITED STATES OF AMERICA

INTRODUCTION

THESE chapters, for the most part, are reprinted from Lafcadio Hearn's "Interpretations of Literature," 1915, from his "Life and Literature," 1916, and from his "Appreciations of Poetry," 1917. Three chapters appear here for the first time. They are all taken from the student notes of Hearn's lectures at the University of Tokyo, 1896-1902, sufficiently described in the earlier volumes just mentioned. They are now published in this regrouping in response to a demand for a further selection of the lectures, in a less expensive volume and with emphasis upon those papers which illustrate Hearn's extraordinary ability to interpret the exotic in life and in books.

It should be remembered that these lectures were delivered to Japanese students, and that Hearn's purpose was not only to impart the information about Western literature usually to be found in our histories and text-books, but much more to explain to the Oriental mind those peculiarities of our civilization which might be hard to understand on the further side of the Pacific Ocean. The lectures are therefore unique, in that they are the first large attempt by a Western critic to interpret us to the East. That we shall be deeply concerned in the near future to continue this interpretation on an even larger scale, no one of us doubts. We wish we might hope for another genius like Hearn to carry on the work.

The merit of the chapters printed or reprinted in the present volume seems to me their power to teach us to imagine our familiar traditions as foreign and exotic in the eyes of other peoples. We are accustomed, like every one else, to think of our literature as the final product of other literatures—as a terminal in itself, rather than as a channel through which great potentialities might flow. Like other men, we are accustomed to think of ourselves as native, under all circumstances, and of other people at all times as foreign. While we were staying in their country, did we not think of the French as foreigners? In these chapters, not originally intended for us, we have the piquant and salutary experience of seeing what we look like on at least one occasion when we are the foreigners; we catch at least a glimpse of what to the Orient seems exotic in us, and it does us no harm to observe that the peculiarly Western aspects of our culture are not self-justifying nor always justifiable when looked at through eyes not already disposed in their favour. Hearn was one of the most loyal advocates the West could possibly have sent to the East, but he was an honest artist, and he never tried to improve his case by trimming a fact. His interpretation of us, therefore, touches our sensitiveness in regions—and in a degree—which perhaps his Japanese students were unconscious of; we too marvel as well as they at his skill in explaining, but we are sensitive to what he found necessary to explain. We read less for the explanation than for the inventory of ourselves.

Any interpretation of life which looks closely to the facts will probably increase our sense of mystery and of strangeness in common things. If on the other hand it is a theory of experience which chiefly interests us, we may divert our attention somewhat from the experience to the theory, leaving the world as humdrum as it was before we explained it. In that case we must seek the exotic in remote places and in exceptional conditions, if we are to observe it at all. But Lafcadio Hearn cultivated in himself and taught his students to cultivate a quick alertness to those qualities of life to which we are usually dulled by habit. Education as he conceived of it had for its purpose what Pater says is the end of philosophy, to rouse the human spirit, to startle it into sharp and eager observation. It is a sign that dulness is already spreading in us, if we must go far afield for the stimulating, the wondrous, the miraculous. The growing sensitiveness of a sound education would help us to distinguish these qualities of romance in the very heart of our daily life. To have so distinguished them is in

my opinion the felicity of Hearn in these chapters.
When he was writing of Japan for European or
American readers, we caught easily enough the
exotic atmosphere of the island kingdom—easily
enough, since it was the essence of a world far
removed from ours. The exotic note is quite as
strong in these chapters. We shall begin to appreciate Hearn's genius when we reflect that here
he finds for us the exotic in ourselves.

The first three chapters deal from different
standpoints with the same subject—the characteristic of Western civilization which to the East is
most puzzling, our attitude toward women.
Hearn attempted in other essays also to do full
justice to this fascinating theme, but these illus-
trations are typical of his method. To the Oriental it is strange to discover a civilization in which
the love of husband and wife altogether super-
sedes the love of children for their parents, yet
this is the civilization he will meet in English and
in most Western literatures. He can understand
the love of individual women, as we understand
the love of individual men, but he will not easily
understand our worship of women as a sex, our
esteem of womankind, our chivalry, our way of
taking woman as a religion. How difficult, then,
will he find such a poem as Tennyson's "Princess,"
or most English novels. He will wonder why
the majority of all Western stories are love
stories, and why in English literature the love

story takes place before marriage, whereas in French and other Continental literatures it usually follows marriage. In Japan marriages are the concern of the parents; with us they are the concern of the lovers, who must choose their mates in competition more or less open with other suitors. No wonder the rivalries and the precarious technique of love-making are with us an obsession quite exotic to the Eastern mind. But the Japanese reader, if he would understand us, must also learn how it is that we have two ways of reckoning with love—a realistic way, which occupies itself in portraying sex, the roots of the tree, as Hearn says, and the idealistic way, which tries to fix and reproduce the beautiful illusion of either happy or unhappy passion. And if the Japanese reader has learned enough of our world to understand all this, he must yet visualize our social system more clearly perhaps than most of us see it, if he would know why so many of our love poems are addressed to the woman we have not yet met. When we begin to sympathize with him in his efforts to grasp the meaning of our literature, we are at last awakened ourselves to some notion of what our civilization means, and as Hearn guides us through the discipline, we realize an exotic quality in things which formerly we took for granted.

Lecturing before the days of Imagism, before the attention of many American poets had been

turned to Japanese art, Hearn recognized the
scarcity in our literature of those short forms of
verse in which the Greeks as well as the Japanese
excel. The epigram with us is—or was until recently—a classical tradition, based on the brief
inscriptions of the Greek anthology or on the
sharp satires of Roman poetry; we had no native
turn for the form as an expression of our contemporary life. Since Hearn gave his very significant lecture we have discovered for ourselves
an American kind of short poem, witty rather
than poetic, and few verse-forms are now practised more widely among us. Hearn spoke as a
prophet or as a shrewd observer—which is the
same thing—when he pointed out the possibility
of development in this field of brevity. He saw
that Japan was closer to the Greek world in this
practice than we were, and that our indifference to
the shorter forms constituted a peculiarity which
we could hardly defend. He saw, also, in the
work of Heredia, how great an influence Japanese
painting might have on Western literature, even
on those poets who had no other acquaintance
with Japan. In this point also his observation
has proved prophetic; the new poets in America
have adopted Japan, as they have adopted Greece,
as a literary theme, and it is somewhat exclusively
from the fine arts of either country that they draw
their idea of its life.

The next chapters which are brought together

here, consider the origin and the nature of English and European ethics. Hearn was an artist
to the core, and as a writer he pursued with undi-
vided purpose that beauty which, as Keats reminded us, is truth. In his creative moments he
was a beauty-lover, not a moralist. But when he
turned critic he at once stressed the cardinal importance of ethics in the study of literature. The
art which strives to end in beauty will reveal even
more clearly than more complex forms of expression the personality of the artist, and personality
is a matter of character, and character both governs the choice of an ethical system and is modified by it. Literary criticism as Hearn practised
it is little interested in theology or in the system
of morals publicly professed; it is, however, profoundly concerned with the ethical principles upon
which the artist actually proceeds, the directions
in which his impulses assert themselves, the ver-
dicts of right and wrong which his temperament
pronounces unconsciously, it may be. Here is the
true revelation of character, Hearn thinks, even
though our habitual and instinctive ethics may
differ widely from the ethics we quite sincerely
profess. Whether we know it or not, we are in
such matters the children of some educational or
philosophical system, which, preached at our ancestors long ago, has come at last to envelop us
with the apparent naturalness of the air we
breathe. It is a spiritual liberation of the first

order, to envisage such an atmosphere as what it truly is, only a system of ethics effectively inculcated, and to compare the principles we live by with those we thought we lived by. Hearn was contriving illumination for the Japanese when he made his great lecture on the "Havamal," identifying in the ancient Northern poem those precepts which laid down later qualities of English character; for the Oriental reader it would be easier to identify the English traits in Thackeray or Dickens or Meredith if he could first consider them in a dogmatic precept. But the lecture gives us, I think, an extraordinary insight into ourselves, a power of self-criticism almost disconcerting as we realize not only the persistence of ethical ideals in the past, but also the possible career of new ethical systems as they may permeate the books written to-day. To what standard will the reader of our contemporary literature be unconsciously moulded? What account will be given of literature a thousand years from now, when a later critic informs himself of our ethics in order to understand more vitally the pages in which he has been brought up?

Partly to inform his Japanese students still further as to our ethical tendencies in literature, and partly I think to indulge his own speculation as to the morality that will be found in the literature of the future, Hearn gave his remarkable lectures on the ant-world, following Fabre and

other European investigators, and his lecture on
"The New Ethics." When he spoke, over twenty
years ago, the socialistic ideal had not gripped us
so effectually as it has done in the last decade, but
he had no difficulty in observing the tendency.
Civilization in some later cycle may wonder at our
ambition to abandon individual liberty and re-
sponsibility and to subside into the social instincts
of the ant; and even as it wonders, that far-off
civilization may detect in itself ant-like reactions
which we cultivated for it. With this description
of the ant-world it is illuminating to read the two
brilliant chapters on English and French poems
about insects. Against this whole background of
ethical theory, I have ventured to set Hearn's
singularly objective account of the Bible.

In the remaining four chapters Hearn speaks of
the "Kalevala," of the mediæval romance "Amis
and Amile," of William Cory's "Ionica," and of
Theocritus. These chapters deal obviously with
literary influences which have become part and
parcel of English poetry, yet which remain exotic
to it, if we keep in mind the Northern stock which
still gives character, ethical and otherwise, to the
English tradition. The "Kalevala," which otherwise should seem nearest to the basic qualities of
our poetry, is almost unique, as Hearn points out,
in the extent of its preoccupation with enchant-
ments and charms, with the magic of words.
"Amis and Amile," which otherwise ought to seem

more foreign to us, is strangely close in its glori-
fication of friendship; for chivalry left with us at
least this one great ethical feeling, that to keep
faith in friendship is a holy thing. No wonder
Amicus and Amelius were popular saints. The
story implies also, as it falls here in the book,
some illustration of those unconscious or uncon-
sidered ethical reactions which, as we saw in the
chapter on the "Havamal," have a lasting influence
on our ideals and on our conduct.

Romanticist though he was, Hearn constantly
sought the romance in the highway of life, the
aspects of experience which seem to perpetuate
themselves from age to age, compelling literature
to reassert them under whatever changes of form.
To one who has followed the large mass of his
lectures it is not surprising that he emphasized
those ethical positions which are likely to remain
constant, in spite of much new philosophy, nor
that he constantly recurred to such books as Cory's
"Ionica," or Lang's translation of Theocritus, in
which he found statements of enduring human
attitudes. To him the Greek mind made a double
appeal. Not only did it represent to him the best
that has yet been thought or said in the world, but
by its fineness and its maturity it seemed kindred
to the spirit he found in ancient Japan. Lecturing to Japanese students on Greek poetry as it
filters through English paraphrases and translations, he must have felt sometimes as we now feel

in reading his lectures, that in his teaching the long
migration of the world's culture was approaching
the end of the circuit, and that the earliest apparition of the East known to most of us was once
more arriving at its starting place, mystery returning to mystery, and its path at all points mysterious, if we rightly observe the miracle of the human
spirit.

CONTENTS

BOOKS AND HABITS

BOOKS AND HABITS

CHAPTER I

THE INSUPERABLE DIFFICULTY

I wish to speak of the greatest difficulty with which the Japanese students of English literature, or of almost any Western literature, have to contend. I do not think that it ever has been properly spoken about. A foreign teacher might well hesitate to speak about it—because, if he should try to explain it merely from the Western point of view, he could not hope to be understood; and if he should try to speak about it from the Japanese point of view, he would be certain to make various mistakes and to utter various extravagances. The proper explanation might be given by a Japanese professor only, who should have so intimate an acquaintance with Western life as to sympathize with it. Yet I fear that it would be difficult to find such a Japanese professor for this reason, that just in proportion as he should find himself in sympathy with Western life, in that proportion he would become less and less able to communicate that sympathy to his students. The difficulties are so great that it has taken me many years even to partly guess how great they are.

That they can be removed at the present day is utterly out of the question. But something may be gained by stating them even imperfectly. At the risk of making blunders and uttering extravagances, I shall make the attempt. I am impelled to do so by a recent conversation with one of the cleverest students that I ever had, who acknowledged his total inability to understand some of the commonest facts in Western life,—all those facts relating, directly or indirectly, to the position of woman in Western literature as reflecting Western life.

Let us clear the ground at once by putting down some facts in the plainest and lowest terms possible. You must try to imagine a country in which the place of the highest virtue is occupied, so to speak, by the devotion of sex to sex. The highest duty of the man is not to his father, but to his wife; and for the sake of that woman he abandons all other earthly ties, should any of these happen to interfere with that relation. The first duty of the wife may be, indeed, must be, to her child, when she has one; but otherwise her husband is her divinity and king. In that country it would be thought unnatural or strange to have one's parents living in the same house with wife or husband. You know all this. But it does not explain for you other things, much more difficult to understand, especially the influence of the abstract idea of woman upon society at large as well as upon the conduct of the individual. The devotion of man to woman does not mean at all only the devotion of husband to wife. It means actually this, —that every man is bound by conviction and by opinion to put all women before himself, simply because they are women. I do not mean that any man is likely to think of any woman as being his intellectual and physical superior; but I do mean that he is bound to think of her as something deserving and needing the help of every man. In time of danger the woman must be saved first. In time of pleasure, the woman must be given the best place. In time of hardship the woman's share of the common pain must be taken voluntarily by the man as much as possible. This is not with any view to recognition of the kindness shown. The man who assists a woman in danger is not supposed to have any claim upon her for that reason. He has done his duty only, not to her, the individual, but to womankind at large. So we have arrived at this general fact, that the first place in all things, except rule, is given to woman in Western countries, and that it is given almost religiously.

Is woman a religion? Well, perhaps you will have the chance of judging for yourselves if you go to America. There you will find men treating women with just the same respect formerly accorded only to religious dignitaries or to great nobles. Everywhere they are saluted and helped to the best places; everywhere they are treated as superior beings. Now if we find reverence, loyalty and all kinds of sacrifices devoted either to a human being or to an image, we are inclined to think of worship. And worship it is. If a Western man should hear me tell you this, he would want the statement qualified, unless he happened to be a philosopher. But I am trying to put the facts before you in the way in which you can best understand them. Let me say, then, that the all-important thing for the student of English literature to try to understand, is that in Western countries woman is a cult, a religion, or if you like still plainer language, I shall say that in Western countries woman is a god.

So much for the abstract idea of woman. Probably you will not find that particularly strange; the idea is not altogether foreign to Eastern thought, and there are very extensive systems of feminine pantheism in India. Of course the Western idea is only in the romantic sense a feminine pantheism; but the Oriental idea may serve to render it more comprehensive. The ideas of divine Mother and divine Creator may be studied in a thousand forms; I am now referring rather to the sentiment, to the feeling, than to the philosophical conception.

You may ask, if the idea or sentiment of divinity attaches to woman in the abstract, what about woman in the concrete—individual woman?

Are women individually considered as gods? Well, that depends on how you define the word god. The following definition would cover the ground, I think:—"Gods are beings superior to man, capable of assisting or injuring him, and to be placated by sacrifice and prayer." Now according to this definition, I think that the attitude of man towards woman in Western countries might be very well characterized as a sort of worship. In the upper classes of society, and in the middle classes also, great reverence towards women is exacted. Men bow down before them, make all kinds of sacrifices to please them, beg for their good will and their assistance. It does not matter that this sacrifice is not in the shape of incense burning or of temple offerings; nor does it matter that the prayers are of a different kind from those pronounced in churches. There is sacrifice and worship. And no saying is more common, no truth better known, than that the man who hopes to succeed in life must be able to please the women. Every young man who goes into any kind of society knows this. It is one of the first lessons that he has to learn. Well, am I very wrong in saying that the attitude of men towards women in the West is much like the attitude of men towards gods?

But you may answer at once,—How comes it, if women are thus reverenced as you say, that men of the lower classes beat and ill-treat their wives in those countries? I must reply, for the same reason that Italian and Spanish sailors will beat and abuse the images of the saints and virgins to whom they pray, when their prayer is not granted. It is quite possible to worship an image sincerely, and to seek vengeance upon it in a moment of anger. The one feeling does not exclude the other. What in the higher classes may be a religion, in the lower classes may be only a superstition, and strange contradictions exist, side by side, in all forms of superstition. Certainly the Western working man or peasant does not think about his wife or his neighbour's wife in the reverential way that the man of the superior class does. But you will find, if you talk to them, that something of the reverential idea is there; it is there at least during their best moments.

Now there is a certain exaggeration in what I have said. But that is only because of the somewhat narrow way in which I have tried to express a truth. I am anxious to give you the idea that throughout the West there exists, though with a difference according to class and culture, a sentiment about women quite as reverential as a sentiment of religion. This is true; and not to understand it, is not to understand Western literature.

How did it come into existence? Through many causes, some of which are so old that we can not know anything about them. This feeling did not belong to the Greek and Roman civiliza-

tion, but it belonged to the life of the old Northern races, who have since spread over the world,
planting their ideas everywhere.   In the oldest
Scandinavian literature you will find that women
were thought of and treated by the men of the
North very much as they are thought of and
treated by Englishmen of to-day. You will find
what their power was in the old sagas, such as the
Njal-Saga, or "The Story of Burnt Njal." But
we must go much further than the written literature to get a full knowledge of the origin of such
a sentiment. The idea seems to have existed that
woman was semi-divine, because she was the
mother, the creator of man. And we know that
she was credited among the Norsemen with supernatural powers. But upon this Northern foundation there was built up a highly complex fabric of
romantic and artistic sentiment. The Christian
worship of the Virgin Mary harmonized with the
Northern belief. The sentiment of chivalry re-
inforced it. Then came the artistic resurrection of
the Renaissance, and the new reverence for the
beauty of the old Greek gods, and the Greek traditions of female divinities; these also coloured
and lightened the old feeling about womankind.
Think also of the effect with which literature,
poetry and the arts have since been cultivating
and developing the sentiment. Consider how the
great mass of Western poetry is love poetry, and
the greater part of Western fiction love stories.

Of course the foregoing is only the vaguest suggestion of a truth. Really my object is not to trouble you at all about the evolutional history of the sentiment, but only to ask you to think what this sentiment means in literature. I am not asking you to sympathize with it, but if you could sympathize with it you would understand a thousand things in Western books which otherwise must remain dim and strange. I am not expecting that you can sympathize with it. But it is absolutely necessary that you should understand its relation to language and literature. Therefore I have to tell you that you should try to think of it as a kind of religion, a secular, social, artistic religion, not to be confounded with any national religion. It is a kind of race feeling or race creed. It has not originated in any sensuous idea, but in some very ancient superstitious idea. Nearly all forms of the highest sentiment and the highest faith and the highest art have had their beginnings in equally humble soil.

CHAPTER II

ON LOVE IN ENGLISH POETRY

I OFTEN imagine that the longer he studies English literature the more the Japanese student must be astonished at the extraordinary predominance given to the passion of love both in fiction and in poetry. Indeed, by this time I have begun to feel a little astonished at it myself. Of course, before I came to this country it seemed to me quite natural that love should be the chief subject of literature; because I did not know anything about any other kind of society except Western society. But to-day it really seems to me a little strange. If it seems strange to me, how much more ought it to seem strange to you! Of course, the simple explanation of the fact is that marriage is the most important act of man's life in Europe or America, and that everything depends upon it. It is quite different on this side of the world. But the simple explanation of the difference is not enough. There are many things to be explained. Why should not only the novel writers but all the poets make love the principal subject of their work? I never knew, because I never thought, how much English literature was saturated with the subject of love until I attempted to make selections of poetry and prose for class use—naturally endeavouring to select such pages or poems as related to other subjects than passion. Instead of finding a good deal of what I was looking for, I could find scarcely anything. The great prose writers, outside of the essay or history, are nearly all famous as tellers of love stories. And it is almost impossible to select half a dozen stanzas of classic verse from Tennyson or Rossetti or Browning or Shelley or Byron, which do not contain anything about kissing, embracing, or longing for some imaginary or real beloved. Wordsworth, indeed, is something of an exception; and Coleridge is most famous for a poem which contains nothing at all about love. But exceptions do not affect the general rule that love is the theme of English poetry, as it is also of French, Italian, Spanish, or German poetry. It is the dominant motive.

So with the English novelists. There have been here also a few exceptions—such as the late Robert Louis Stevenson, most of whose novels contain little about women; they are chiefly novels or romances of adventure. But the exceptions are very few. At the present time there are produced almost every year in England about a thousand new novels, and all of these or nearly all are love stories. To write a novel without a woman in it would be a dangerous undertaking; in ninety-nine cases out of a hundred the book would not sell.

Of course all this means that the English people throughout the world, as readers, are chiefly interested in the subject under discussion. When you find a whole race interested more in one thing than in anything else, you may be sure that it is so because the subject is of paramount importance in the life of the average person. You must try to imagine then, a society in which every man must choose his wife, and every woman must choose her husband, independent of all outside help, and not only choose but obtain if possible. The great principle of Western society is that competition rules here as it rules in everything else. The best man—that is to say, the strongest and cleverest— is likely to get the best woman, in the sense of the most beautiful person. The weak, the feeble, the poor, and the ugly have little chance of being able to marry at all. Tens of thousands of men and women can not possibly marry. I am speaking of the upper and middle classes. The working people, the peasants, the labourers, these marry young; but the competition there is just the same—just as difficult, and only a little rougher. So it may be said that every man has a struggle of some kind in order to marry, and that there is a kind of fight or contest for the possession of every woman worth having. Taking this view of Western society not only in England but throughout all Europe, you will easily be able to see why the Western public have reason to be more interested in literature which treats of love than in any other kind of literature.

But although the conditions that I have been describing are about the same in all Western countries, the tone of the literature which deals with love is not at all the same. There are very great differences. In prose they are much more serious than in poetry; because in all countries a man is allowed, by public opinion, more freedom in verse than in prose. Now these differences in the way of treating the subject in different countries really indicate national differences of character. Northern love stories and Northern poetry about love are very serious; and these authors are kept within fixed limits. Certain subjects are generally forbidden. For example, the English public wants novels about love, but the love must be the love of a girl who is to become somebody's wife. The rule in the English novel is to describe the pains, fears, and struggles of the period before marriage—the contest in the world for the right of marriage. A man must not write a novel about any other point of love. Of course there are plenty of authors who have broken this rule, but the rule still exists. A man may represent a contest between two women, one good and one bad, but if the bad woman is allowed to conquer in the story, the public will growl. This English fashion has existed since the eighteenth century,

since the time of Richardson, and is likely to last
for generations to come.

Now this is not the rule at all which governs
the making of novels in France. French novels
generally treat of the relations of women to the
world and to lovers, after marriage; consequently
there is a great deal in French novels about adultery, about improper relations between the sexes,
about many things which the English public would
not allow. This does not mean that the English
are morally a better people than the French or
other Southern races. But it does mean that there
are great differences in the social conditions. One
such difference can be very briefly expressed. An
English girl, an American girl, a Norwegian, a
Dane, a Swede, is allowed all possible liberty before marriage. The girl is told, "You must be
able to take care of yourself, and not do wrong."
After marriage there is no more such liberty.
After marriage in all Northern countries a woman's conduct is strictly watched. But in France,
and in Southern countries, the young girl has no
liberty before marriage. She is always under the
guard of her brother, her father, her mother, or
some experienced relation. She is accompanied
wherever she walks. She is not allowed to see
her betrothed except in the presence of witnesses.
But after marriage her liberty begins. Then she
is told for the first time that she must take care of

herself. Well, you will see that the conditions
which inspire the novels, in treating of the subject
of love and marriage, are very different in Northern and in Southern Europe. For this reason
alone the character of the novel produced in
England could not be the same.

You must remember, however, that there are
many other reasons for this difference—reasons
of literary sentiment. The Southern or Latin
races have been civilized for a much longer time
than the Northern races; they have inherited the
feelings of the ancient world, the old Greek and
Roman world, and they think still about the relation of the sexes in very much the same way that
the ancient poets and romance writers used to
think. And they can do things which English
writers can not do, because their language has
power of more delicate expression.

We may say that the Latin writers still speak
of love in very much the same way that it was
considered before Christianity. But when I speak
of Christianity I am only referring to an historical
date. Before Christianity the Northern races also
thought about love very much in the same way
that their best poets do at this day. The ancient
Scandinavian literature would show this. The
Viking, the old sea-pirate, felt very much as Tennyson or as Meredith would feel upon this subject; he thought of only one kind of love as real—
that which ends in marriage, the affection between

husband and wife. Anything else was to him mere folly and weakness. Christianity did not change his sentiment on this subject. The modern Englishman, Swede, Dane, Norwegian, or German regards love in exactly that deep, serious, noble way that his pagan ancestors did. I think we can say that different races have differences of feeling on sexual relations, which differences are very much older than any written history. They are in the blood and soul of a people, and neither religion nor civilization can utterly change them.

So far I have been speaking particularly about the differences in English and French novels; and a novel is especially a reflection of national life, a kind of dramatic narration of truth, in the form of a story. But in poetry, which is the highest form of literature, the difference is much more observable. We find the Latin poets of to-day writing just as freely on the subject of love as the old Latin poets of the age of Augustus, while Northern poets observe with few exceptions great restraint when treating of this theme. Now where is the line to be drawn? Are the Latins right? Are the English right? How are we to make a sharp distinction between what is moral and good and what is immoral and bad in treating love-subjects?

Some definition must be attempted.

What is meant by love? As used by Latin writers the word has a range of meanings, from that of the sexual relation between insects or animals up to the highest form of religious emotion, called "The love of God." I need scarcely say that this definition is too loose for our use. The English word, by general consent, means both sexual passion and deep friendship. This again is a meaning too wide for our purpose. By putting the adjective "true" before love, some definition is attempted in ordinary conversation. When an Englishman speaks of "true love," he usually means something that has no passion at all; he means a perfect friendship which grows up between man and wife and which has nothing to do with the passion which brought the pair together. But when the English poet speaks of love, he generally means passion, not friendship. I am only stating very general rules. You see how confusing the subject is, how difficult to define the matter. Let us leave the definition alone for a moment, and consider the matter philosophically.

Some very foolish persons have attempted even within recent years to make a classification of different kinds of love—love between the sexes. They talk about romantic love, and other such things. All that is utter nonsense. In the meaning of sexual affection there is only one kind of love, the natural attraction of one sex for the other; and the only difference in the highest form of this attraction and the lowest is this, that in the nobler nature a vast number of moral, æsthetic, and ethical sentiments are related to the passion, and that in lower natures those sentiments are absent. Therefore we may say that even in the highest forms of the sentiment there is only one dominant feeling, complex though it be, the desire for possession. What follows the possession we may call love if we please; but it might better be called perfect friendship and sympathy. It is altogether a different thing. The love that is the theme of poets in all countries is really love, not the friendship that grows out of it.

I suppose you know that the etymological meaning of "passion" is "a state of suffering." In regard to love, the word has particular significance to the Western mind, for it refers to the time of struggle and doubt and longing before the object is attained. Now how much of this passion is a legitimate subject of literary art?

The difficulty may, I think, be met by remembering the extraordinary character of the mental phenomena which manifest themselves in the time of passion. There is during that time a strange illusion, an illusion so wonderful that it has engaged the attention of great philosophers for thousands of years; Plato, you know, tried to explain it in a very famous theory. I mean the illusion that seems to charm, or rather, actually does charm the senses of a man at a certain time.

To his eye a certain face has suddenly become the most beautiful object in the world. To his ears the accents of one voice become the sweetest of all music. Reason has nothing to do with this, and reason has no power against the enchantment. Out of Nature's mystery, somehow or other, this strange magic suddenly illuminates the senses of a man; then vanishes again, as noiselessly as it came. It is a very ghostly thing, and can not be explained by any theory not of a very ghostly kind. Even Herbert Spencer has devoted his reasoning to a new theory about it. I need not go further in this particular than to tell you that in a certain way passion is now thought to have something to do with other lives than the present; in short, it is a kind of organic memory of relations that existed in thousands and tens of thousands of former states of being. Right or wrong though the theories may be, this mysterious moment of love, the period of this illusion, is properly the subject of high poetry, simply because it is the most beautiful and the most wonderful experience of a human life. And why?

Because in the brief time of such passion the very highest and finest emotions of which human nature is capable are brought into play. In that time more than at any other hour in life do men become unselfish, unselfish at least toward one human being. Not only unselfishness but self-sacrifice is a desire peculiar to the period. The young man in love is not merely willing to give away everything that he possesses to the person beloved; he wishes to suffer pain, to meet danger, to risk his life for her sake. Therefore Tennyson, in speaking of that time, beautifully said:

Love took up the harp of Life, and smote on all the chords
  with might,
Smote the chord of Self, that, trembling, pass'd in music
  out of sight.

Unselfishness is, of course, a very noble feeling, independently of the cause. But this is only one of the emotions of a higher class when powerfully aroused. There is pity, tenderness—the same kind of tenderness that one feels toward a child—the love of the helpless, the desire to protect. And a third sentiment felt at such a time more strongly than at any other, is the sentiment of duty; responsibilities moral and social are then comprehended in a totally new way. Surely none can dispute these facts nor the beauty of them.

Moral sentiments are the highest of all; but next to them the sentiment of beauty in itself, the artistic feeling, is also a very high form of intellectual and even of secondary moral experience. Scientifically there is a relation between the beautiful and the good, between the physically perfect and the ethically perfect. Of course it is not absolute. There is nothing absolute in this world. But the relation exists. Whoever can comprehend the highest form of one kind of beauty must be able to comprehend something of the other. I know very well that the ideal of the love-season is an illusion; in nine hundred and ninety-nine cases out of the thousand the beauty of the woman is only imagined. But does that make any possible difference? I do not think that it does. To imagine beauty is really to see it—not objectively, perhaps, but subjectively beyond all possibility of doubt. Though you see the beauty only in your mind, in your mind it is; and in your mind its ethical influence must operate. During the time that a man worships even imaginary bodily beauty, he receives some secret glimpse of a higher kind of beauty—beauty of heart and mind. Was there ever in this world a real lover who did not believe the woman of his choice to be not only the most beautiful of mortals, but also the best in a moral sense? I do not think that there ever was.

The moral and the ethical sentiments of a being thus aroused call into sudden action all the finer energies of the man—the capacities for effort, for heroism, for high-pressure work of any sort, mental or physical, for all that requires quickness in thought and exactitude in act. There is for the time being a sense of new power. Anything that makes strong appeal to the best exercise of one's faculties is beneficent and, in most cases, worthy of reverence. Indeed, it is in the short season of which I am speaking that we always discover the best of everything in the character of woman or of man. In that period the evil qualities, the ungenerous side, is usually kept as much out of sight as possible.

Now for all these suggested reasons, as for many others which might be suggested, the period of illusion in love is really the period which poets and writers of romance are naturally justified in describing. Can they go beyond it with safety, with propriety? That depends very much upon whether they go up or down. By going up I mean keeping within the region of moral idealism. By going down I mean descending to the level of merely animal realism. In this realism there is nothing deserving the highest effort of art of any sort.

What is the object of art? Is it not, or should it not be, to make us imagine better conditions than that which at present exist in the world, and by so imagining to prepare the way for the coming of such conditions? I think that all great art has done this. Do you remember the old story about Greek mothers keeping in their rooms the statue of a god or a man, more beautiful than anything real, so that their imagination might be constantly influenced by the sight of beauty, and that they might perhaps be able to bring more beautiful children into the world? Among the Arabs, mothers also do something of this kind, only, as

they have no art of imagery, they go to Nature
herself for the living image. Black luminous eyes
are beautiful, and wives keep in their tents a little
deer, the gazelle, which is famous for the bril-
liancy and beauty of its eyes. By constantly looking at this charming pet the Arab wife hopes to
bring into the world some day a child with eyes
as beautiful as the eyes of the gazelle. Well, the
highest function of art ought to do for us, or at
least for the world, what the statue and the gazelle were expected to do for Grecian and Arab
mothers—to make possible higher conditions than
the existing ones.

So much being said, consider again the place
and the meaning of the passion of love in any
human life. It is essentially a period of idealism,
of imagining better things and conditions than are
possible in this world. For everybody who has
been in love has imagined something higher than
the possible and the present. Any idealism is a
proper subject for art. It is not at all the same
in the case of realism. Grant that all this passion,
imagination, and fine sentiment is based upon a
very simple animal impulse. That does not make
the least difference in the value of the highest results of that passion. We might say the very same
thing about any human emotion; every emotion
can be evolutionally traced back to simple and selfish impulses shared by man with the lower animals. But because an apple tree or a pear tree

happens to have its roots in the ground, does that
mean that its fruits are not beautiful and whole-
some? Most assuredly we must not judge the
fruit of the tree from the unseen roots; but what
about turning up the ground to look at the roots?
What becomes of the beauty of the tree when you
do that? The realist—at least the French realist
—likes to do that. He likes to bring back the
attention of his reader to the lowest rather than
to the highest, to that which should be kept hidden, for the very same reason that the roots of
a tree should be kept underground if the tree is
to live.

The time of illusion, then, is the beautiful moment of passion; it represents the artistic zone in
which the poet or romance writer ought to be free
to do the very best that he can. He may go beyond that zone; but then he has only two directions in which he can travel. Above it there is
religion, and an artist may, like Dante, succeed in
transforming love into a sentiment of religious
ecstasy. I do not think that any artist could do
that to-day; this is not an age of religious ecstasy.
But upwards there is no other way to go. Downwards the artist may travel until he finds himself
in hell. Between the zone of idealism and the
brutality of realism there are no doubt many gra-
dations. I am only indicating what I think to be
an absolute truth, that in treating of love the
literary master should keep to the period of illu-

sion, and that to go below it is a dangerous undertaking. And now, having tried to make what are
believed to be proper distinctions between great
literature on this subject and all that is not great,
we may begin to study a few examples. I am
going to select at random passages from English
poets and others, illustrating my meaning.

Tennyson is perhaps the most familiar to you
among poets of our own time; and he has given a
few exquisite examples of the ideal sentiment in
passion. One is a concluding verse in the beautiful song that occurs in the monodrama of
"Maud," where the lover, listening in the garden,
hears the steps of his beloved approaching.

> She is coming, my own, my sweet,
>   Were it ever so airy a tread,
> My heart would hear her and beat,
>   Were it earth in an earthy bed;
> My dust would hear her and beat,
>   Had I lain for a century dead;
> Would start and tremble under her feet,
>   And blossom in purple and red.

This is a very fine instance of the purely ideal
emotion—extravagant, if you like, in the force of
the imagery used, but absolutely sincere and true;
for the imagination of love is necessarily extravagant. It would be quite useless to ask whether
the sound of a girl's footsteps could really waken
a dead man; we know that love can fancy such
things quite naturally, not in one country only but

everywhere. An Arabian poem written long before the time of Mohammed contains exactly the same thought in simpler words; and I think that there are some old Japanese songs containing something similar. All that the statement really means is that the voice, the look, the touch, even the footstep of the woman beloved have come to possess for the lover a significance as great as life and death. For the moment he knows no other divinity; she is his god, in the sense that her power over him has become infinite and irresistible.

The second example may be furnished from another part of the same composition—the little song of exaltation after the promise to marry has been given.

O let the solid ground
  Not fail beneath my feet
Before my life has found
  What some have found so sweet;
Then let come what come may,
What matter if I go mad,
I shall have had my day.

Let the sweet heavens endure,
  Not close and darken above me
Before I am quite, quite sure
  That there is one to love me;
Then let come what come may
To a life that has been so sad,
I shall have had my day.

The feeling of the lover is that no matter what happens afterwards, the winning of the woman is enough to pay for life, death, pain, or anything else. One of the most remarkable phenomena of the illusion is the supreme indifference to consequences—at least to any consequences which would not signify moral shame or loss of honour. Of course the poet is supposed to consider the emotion only in generous natures. But the subject of this splendid indifference has been more wonderfully treated by Victor Hugo than by Tennyson—as we shall see later on, when considering another phase of the emotion. Before doing that, I want to call your attention to a very charming treatment of love's romance by an American. It is one of the most delicate of modern compositions, and it is likely to become a classic, as it has already been printed in four or five different anthologies. The title is "Atalanta's Race."

First let me tell you the story of Atalanta, so that you will be better able to see the fine symbolism of the poem. Atalanta, the daughter of a Greek king, was not only the most beautiful of maidens, but the swiftest runner in the world. She passed her time in hunting, and did not wish to marry. But as many men wanted to marry her, a law was passed that any one who desired to win her must run a race with her. If he could beat her in running, then she promised to marry him, but if he lost the race, he was to be killed. Some

say that the man was allowed to run first, and
that the girl followed with a spear in her hand
and killed him when she overtook him. There
are different accounts of the contest. Many
suitors lost the race and were killed. But finally
a young man called Hippomenes obtained from
the Goddess of Love three golden apples, and he
was told that if he dropped these apples while
running, the girl would stop to pick them up, and
that in this way he might be able to win the race.
So he ran, and when he found himself about to
be beaten, he dropped one apple. She stopped to
pick it up and thus he gained a little. In this way
he won the race and married Atalanta. Greek
mythology says that afterwards she and her husband were turned into lions because they offended
the gods; however, that need not concern us here.
There is a very beautiful moral in the old Greek
story, and the merit of the American composition is that its author, Maurice Thompson, perceived this moral and used it to illustrate a great
philosophical truth.

> When Spring grows old, and sleepy winds
>   Set from the South with odours sweet,
> I see my love, in green, cool groves,
>   Speed down dusk aisles on shining feet.
> She throws a kiss and bids me run,
>   In whispers sweet as roses' breath;
> I know I cannot win the race,
>   And at the end, I know, is death.

But joyfully I bare my limbs,
  Anoint me with the tropic breeze,
And feel through every sinew run
  The vigour of Hippomenes.

O race of love! we all have run
  Thy happy course through groves of Spring,
And cared not, when at last we lost,
  For life or death, or anything!

There are a few thoughts here requiring a little comment. You know that the Greek games and athletic contests were held in the fairest season, and that the contestants were stripped. They were also anointed with oil, partly to protect the skin against sun and temperature and partly to make the body more supple. The poet speaks of the young man as being anointed by the warm wind of Spring, the tropic season of life. It is a very pretty fancy. What he is really telling us is this:

"There are no more Greek games, but the race of love is still run to-day as in times gone by; youth is the season, and the atmosphere of youth is the anointing of the contestant."

But the moral of the piece is its great charm, the poetical statement of a beautiful and a wonderful fact. In almost every life there is a time when we care for only one person, and suffer much for that person's sake; yet in that period we do not care whether we suffer or die, and in after life, when we look back at those hours of youth, we wonder at the way in which we then felt. In European life of to-day the old Greek fable is still true; almost everybody must run Atalanta's race and abide by the result.

One of the delightful phases of the illusion of love is the sense of old acquaintance, the feeling as if the person loved had been known and loved long ago in some time and place forgotten. I think you must have observed, many of you, that when the senses of sight and hearing happen to be strongly stirred by some new and most pleasurable experience, the feeling of novelty is absent, or almost absent. You do not feel as if you were seeing or hearing something new, but as if you saw or heard something that you knew all about very long ago. I remember once travelling with a Japanese boy into a charming little country town in Shikoku—and scarcely had we entered the main street, than he cried out: "Oh, I have seen this place before!" Of course he had not seen it before; he was from Osaka and had never left the great city until then. But the pleasure of his new experience had given him this feeling of familiarity with the unfamiliar. I do not pretend to explain this familiarity with the new—it is a great mystery still, just as it was a great mystery to the Roman Cicero. But almost everybody that has been in love has probably had the same feeling during a moment or two—the feeling "I have

known that woman before," though the where
and the when are mysteries. Some of the modern
poets have beautifully treated this feeling. The
best example that I can give you is the exquisite
lyric by Rossetti entitled "Sudden Light."

> I have been here before,
>   But when or how I cannot tell:
> I know the grass beyond the door,
>   The sweet keen smell,
> The sighing sound, the lights around the shore.
>
> You have been mine before,—
>   How long ago I may not know:
> But just when at that swallow's soar
>   Your neck turn'd so,
> Some veil did fall,—I knew it all of yore.
>
> Has this been thus before?
>   And shall not thus time's eddying flight
> Still with our lives our loves restore
>   In death's despite,
> And day and night yield one delight once more?

I think you will acknowledge that this is very
pretty; and the same poet has treated the idea
equally well in other poems of a more complicated
kind. But another poet of the period was haunted
even more than Rossetti by this idea—Arthur
O'Shaughnessy. Like Rossetti he was a great
lover, and very unfortunate in his love; and he
wrote his poems, now famous, out of the pain and

regret that was in his heart, much as singing birds
born in cages are said to sing better when their
eyes are put out. Here is one example:

Along the garden ways just now
I heard the flowers speak;
The white rose told me of your brow,
The red rose of your cheek;
The lily of your bended head,
The bindweed of your hair:
Each looked its loveliest and said
You were more fair.

I went into the woods anon,
And heard the wild birds sing
How sweet you were; they warbled on,
Piped, trill'd the self-same thing.
Thrush, blackbird, linnet, without pause
The burden did repeat,
And still began again because
You were more sweet.

And then I went down to the sea,
And heard it murmuring too,
Part of an ancient mystery,
All made of me and you:
How many a thousand years ago
I loved, and you were sweet—
Longer I could not stay, and so
I fled back to your feet.

The last stanza especially expresses the idea
that I have been telling you about; but in a poem

entitled "Greater Memory" the idea is much more
fully expressed. By "greater memory" you must
understand the memory beyond this life into past
stages of existence. This piece has become a part
of the nineteenth century poetry that will live;
and a few of the best stanzas deserve to be quoted.

In the heart there lay buried for years
Love's story of passion and tears;
Of the heaven that two had begun
    And the horror that tore them apart;
When one was love's slayer, but one
    Made a grave for the love in his heart.

The long years pass'd weary and lone
And it lay there and changed there unknown;
Then one day from its innermost place,
    In the shamed and ruin'd love's stead,
Love arose with a glorified face,
    Like an angel that comes from the dead.

It uplifted the stone that was set
On that tomb which the heart held yet;
But the sorrow had moulder'd within.
    And there came from the long closed door
A dear image, that was not the sin
    Or the grief that lay buried before.

.   .   .   .   .

There was never the stain of a tear
On the face that was ever so dear;
'Twas the same in each lovelier way;
    'Twas old love's holier part,
And the dream of the earliest day
    Brought back to the desolate heart.

It was knowledge of all that had been
In the thought, in the soul unseen;
'Twas the word which the lips could not say
    To redeem or recover the past.
It was more than was taken away
    Which the heart got back at the last.

The passion that lost its spell,
The rose that died where it fell,
The look that was look'd in vain,
    The prayer that seemed lost evermore,
They were found in the heart again,
    With all that the heart would restore.

Put into less mystical language the legend is
this: A young man and a young woman loved
each other for a time; then they were separated
by some great wrong—we may suppose the
woman was untrue. The man always loved her
memory, in spite of this wrong which she had
done. The two died and were buried; hundreds
and hundreds of years they remained buried, and
the dust of them mixed with the dust of the earth.
But in the perpetual order of things, a pure love
never can die, though bodies may die and pass
away. So after many generations the pure love
which this man had for a bad woman was born
again in the heart of another man—the same, yet
not the same. And the spirit of the woman that
long ago had done the wrong, also found incar-
nation again; and the two meeting, are drawn
to each other by what people call love, but what

is really Greater Memory, the recollection of past
lives. But now all is happiness for them, because
the weaker and worse part of each has really died
and has been left hundreds of years behind, and
only the higher nature has been born again. All
that ought not to have been is not; but all that
ought to be now is. This is really an evolutionary
teaching, but it is also poetical license, for the
immoral side of mankind does not by any means
die so quickly as the poet supposes. It is perhaps
a question of many tens of thousands of years to
get rid of a few of our simpler faults. Anyway,
the fancy charms us and tempts us really to hope
that these things might be so.

While the poets of our time so extend the history of a love backwards beyond this life, we
might expect them to do the very same thing in
the other direction. I do not refer to reunion in
heaven, or anything of that sort, but simply to
affection continued after death. There are some
very pretty fancies of the kind. But they can not
prove to you quite so interesting as the poems
which treat the recollection of past life. When
we consider the past imaginatively, we have some
ground to stand on. The past has been—there is
no doubt about that. The fact that we are at this
moment alive makes it seem sufficiently true that
we were alive thousands or millions of years ago.
But when we turn to the future for poetical inspiration, the case is very different. There we

must imagine without having anything to stand upon in the way of experience. Of course if born again into a body we could imagine many things; but there is the ghostly interval between death and birth which nobody is able to tell us about. Here the poet depends upon dream experiences, and it is of such an experience that Christina Rossetti speaks in her beautiful poem entitled "A Pause."

They made the chamber sweet with flowers and leaves,
    And the bed sweet with flowers on which I lay,
    While my soul, love-bound, loitered on its way.
I did not hear the birds about the eaves,
Nor hear the reapers talk among the sheaves:
Only my soul kept watch from day to day,
    My thirsty soul kept watch for one away:—
Perhaps he loves, I thought, remembers, grieves.

At length there came the step upon the stair,
    Upon the lock the old familiar hand:
Then first my spirit seemed to scent the air
    Of Paradise; then first the tardy sand
Of time ran golden; and I felt my hair
    Put on a glory, and my soul expand.

The woman is dead. In the room where her body died, flowers have been placed, offerings to the dead. Also there are flowers upon the bed. The ghost of the woman observes all this, but she does not feel either glad or sad because of it; she is thinking only of the living lover, who was

not there when she died, but far away. She wants
to know whether he really loved her, whether he
will really be sorry to hear that she is dead. Outside the room of death the birds are singing; in
the fields beyond the windows peasants are working, and talking as they work. But the ghost does
not listen to these sounds. The ghost remains in
the room only for love's sake; she can not go away
until the lover comes. At last she hears him coming. She knows the sound of the step; she knows
the touch of the hand upon the lock of the door.
And instantly, before she sees him at all, she first
feels delight. Already it seems to her that she
can smell the perfume of the flowers of heaven;
it then seems to her that about her head, as about
the head of an angel, a circle of glory is shaping
itself, and the real heaven, the Heaven of Love,
is at hand.

How very beautiful this is. There is still one
line which requires a separate explanation—I
mean the sentence about the sands of time running golden. Perhaps you may remember the
same simile in Tennyson's "Locksley Hall":

Love took up the glass of Time, and turn'd it in his
        glowing hands;
Every moment, lightly shaken, ran itself in golden sands.

Here time is identified with the sand of the hour
glass, and the verb "to run" is used because this
verb commonly expresses the trickling of the sand

from the upper part of the glass into the lower.
In other words, fine sand "runs" just like water.
To say that the sands of time run golden, or
become changed into gold, is only a poetical way
of stating that the time becomes more than happy
—almost heavenly or divine. And now you will
see how very beautiful the comparison becomes in
this little poem about the ghost of the woman
waiting for the coming step of her lover.

Several other aspects of the emotion may now
be considered separately. One of these, an especially beautiful one, is memory. Of course, there
are many aspects of love's memories, some all
happiness, others intensely sorrowful—the memory of a walk, a meeting, a moment of good-bye.
Such memories occupy a very large place in the
treasure house of English love poems. I am going
to give three examples only, but each of a different kind. The first poet that I am going to
mention is Coventry Patmore. He wrote two curious books of poetry, respectively called "The
Angel in the House" and "The Unknown Eros."
In the first of these books he wrote the whole
history of his courtship and marriage—a very
dangerous thing for a poet to do, but he did it
successfully. The second volume is miscellaneous,
and contains some very beautiful things. I am
going to quote only a few lines from the piece
called "Amelia." This piece is the story of an
evening spent with a sweetheart, and the lines

which I am quoting refer to the moment of taking
the girl home. They are now rather famous:

> . . . To the dim street
> I led her sacred feet;
> And so the Daughter gave,
> Soft, moth-like, sweet,
> Showy as damask-rose and shy as musk,
> Back to her Mother, anxious in the dusk.
> And now " Good Night! "

Why should the poet speak of the girl in this
way? Why does he call her feet sacred? She has
just promised to marry him; and now she seems
to him quite divine. But he discovers very plain
words with which to communicate his finer feelings to the reader. The street is "dim" because
it is night; and in the night the beautifully dressed
maiden seems like a splendid moth—the name
given to night butterflies in England. In England
the moths are much more beautiful than the true
butterflies; they have wings of scarlet and purple
and brown and gold. So the comparison, though
peculiarly English, is very fine. Also there is a
suggestion of the soundlessness of the moth's
flight. Now "showy as damask rose" is a striking
simile only because the damask-rose is a wonderfully splendid flower—richest in colour of all roses
in English gardens. "Shy as musk" is rather a
daring simile. "Musk" is a perfume used by
English as well as Japanese ladies, but there is no

perfume which must be used with more discretion, carefulness. If you use ever so little too much, the effect is not pleasant. But if you use exactly the proper quantity, and no more, there is no perfume which is more lovely. "Shy as musk" thus refers to that kind of girlish modesty which never commits a fault even by the measure of a grain— a beautiful shyness incapable of being anything but beautiful. Nevertheless the comparison must be confessed one which should be felt rather than explained.

The second of the three promised quotations shall be from Robert Browning. There is one feeling, not often touched upon by poets, yet peculiar to lovers, that is here treated—the desire when you are very happy or when you are looking at anything attractive to share the pleasure of the moment with the beloved. But it seldom happens that the wish and the conditions really meet. Referring to this longing Browning made a short lyric that is now a classic; it is among the most dainty things of the century.

> Never the time and the place
>   And the loved one all together!
> This path—how soft to pace!
>   This May—what magic weather!
> Where is the loved one's face?
> In a dream that loved one's face meets mine,
> But the house is narrow, the place is bleak
> Where, outside, rain and wind combine

With a furtive ear, if I try to speak,
With a hostile eye at my flushing cheek,
With a malice that marks each word, each sign!

Never can we have things the way we wish in
this world—a beautiful day, a beautiful place, and
the presence of the beloved all at the same time.
Something is always missing; if the place be beautiful, the weather perhaps is bad. Or if the
weather and the place both happen to be perfect,
the woman is absent. So the poet finding himself
in some very beautiful place, and remembering
this, remembers also the last time that he met
the woman beloved. It was a small dark house
and chilly; outside there was rain and storm; and
the sounds of the wind and of the rain were as
the sounds of people secretly listening, or sounds
of people trying to look in secretly through the
windows. Evidently it was necessary that the
meeting should be secret, and it was not altogether
as happy as could have been wished.

The third example is a very beautiful poem; we
must content ourselves with an extract from it.
It is the memory of a betrothal day, and the poet
is Frederick Tennyson. I suppose you know that
there were three Tennysons, and although Alfred
happened to be the greatest, all of them were
good poets.

It is a golden morning of the spring,
My cheek is pale, and hers is warm with bloom,

And we are left in that old carven room,
And she begins to sing;

The open casement quivers in the breeze,
　　And one large musk-rose leans its dewy grace
　　Into the chamber, like a happy face,
And round it swim the bees;

　　　.　　　.　　　.　　　.　　　.　　　.

I know not what I said—what she replied
　　Lives, like eternal sunshine, in my heart;
　　And then I murmured, Oh! we never part,
My love, my life, my bride!

　　　.　　　.　　　.　　　.　　　.　　　.

And silence o'er us, after that great bliss,
　　Fell like a welcome shadow—and I heard
　　The far woods sighing, and a summer bird
Singing amid the trees;

The sweet bird's happy song, that streamed around,
　　The murmur of the woods, the azure skies,
　　Were graven on my heart, though ears and eyes
Marked neither sight nor sound.

She sleeps in peace beneath the chancel stone,
　　But ah! so clearly is the vision seen,
　　The dead seem raised, or Death has never been,
Were I not here alone.

This is great art in its power of picturing a
memory of the heart. Let us notice some of the
beauties. The lover is pale because he is afraid,
anxious; he is going to ask a question and he does
not know how she may answer him. All this was

long ago, years and years ago, but the strong
emotions of that morning leave their every detail
painted in remembrance, with strange vividness.
After all those years the man still recollects the
appearance of the room, the sunshine entering,
and the crimson rose looking into the room from
the garden, with bees humming round it. Then
after the question had been asked and happily
answered, neither could speak for joy; and because of the silence all the sounds of nature outside became almost painfully distinct. Now he
remembers how he heard in that room the sound
of the wind in far-away trees, the singing of a
bird—he also remembers all the colours and the
lights of the day. But it was very, very long ago,
and she is dead. Still, the memory is so clear and
bright in his heart that it is as if time had stood
still, or as if she had come back from the grave.
Only one thing assures him that it is but a memory
—he is alone.

Returning now to the subject of love's illusion
in itself, let me remind you that the illusion does
not always pass away—not at all. It passes away
in every case of happy union, when it has become
no longer necessary to the great purposes of nature. But in case of disappointment, loss, failure
to win the maiden desired, it often happens that
the ideal image never fades away, but persistently
haunts the mind through life, and is capable thus
of making even the most successful life unhappy.

Sometimes the result of such disappointment may be to change all a man's ideas about the world, about life, about religion; and everything remains darkened for him. Many a young person disappointed in love begins to lose religious feeling from that moment, for it seems to him, simply because he happens to be unfortunate, that the universe is all wrong. On the other hand the successful lover thinks that the universe is all right; he utters his thanks to the gods, and feels his faith in religion and human nature greater than before. I do not at this moment remember any striking English poem illustrating this fact; but there is a pretty little poem in French by Victor Hugo showing well the relation between successful love and religious feeling in simple minds. Here is an English translation of it. The subject is simply a walk at night, the girl-bride leaning upon the arm of her husband; and his memory of the evening is thus expressed:

> The trembling arm I pressed
> Fondly; our thoughts confessed
>   Love's conquest tender;
> God filled the vast sweet night,
> Love filled our hearts; the light
>   Of stars made splendour.
>
> Even as we walked and dreamed,
> 'Twixt heaven and earth, it seemed
>   Our souls were speaking;

The stars looked on thy face;
Thine eyes through violet space
    The stars were seeking.

And from the astral light
Feeling the soft sweet night
    Thrill to thy soul,
Thou saidst: " O God of Bliss,
Lord of the Blue Abyss,
    Thou madest the whole! "

And the stars whispered low
To the God of Space, " We know,
    God of Eternity,
Dear Lord, all Love is Thine,
Even by Love's Light we shine!
    Thou madest Beauty! "

Of course here the religious feeling itself is part
of the illusion, but it serves to give great depth
and beauty to simple feeling. Besides, the poem
illustrates one truth very forcibly—namely, that
when we are perfectly happy all the universe appears to be divine and divinely beautiful; in other
words, we are in heaven. On the contrary, when
we are very unhappy the universe appears to be
a kind of hell, in which there is no hope, no joy,
and no gods to pray to.

But the special reason I wished to call attention
to Victor Hugo's lyric is that it has that particular
quality called by philosophical critics "cosmic emotion." Cosmic emotion means the highest quality

of human emotion. The word "cosmos" signifies the universe—not simply this world, but all the hundred millions of suns and worlds in the known heaven. And the adjective "cosmic" means, of course, "related to the whole universe." Ordinary emotion may be more than individual in its relations. I mean that your feelings may be moved by the thought or the perception of something relating not only to your own life but also to the lives of many others. The largest form of such ordinary emotion is what would be called national feeling, the feeling of your own relation to the whole nation or the whole race. But there is higher emotion even than that. When you think of yourself emotionally not only in relation to your own country, your own nation, but in relation to all humanity, then you have a cosmic emotion of the third or second order. I say "third or second," because whether the emotion be second or third rate depends very much upon your conception of humanity as One. But if you think of yourself in relation not to this world only but to the whole universe of hundreds of millions of stars and planets—in relation to the whole mystery of existence—then you have a cosmic emotion of the highest order. Of course there are degrees even in this; the philosopher or the metaphysician will probably have a finer quality of cosmic emotion than the poet or the artist is able to have. But lovers very often, according to their degree

of intellectual culture, experience a kind of cosmic
emotion; and Victor Hugo's little poem illustrates
this. Night and the stars and the abyss of the sky
all seem to be thrilling with love and beauty to
the lover's eyes, because he himself is in a state
of loving happiness; and then he begins to think
about his relation to the universal life, to the supreme mystery beyond all Form and Name.

A third or fourth class of such emotion may be
illustrated by the beautiful sonnet of Keats, written not long before his death. Only a very young
man could have written this, because only a very
young man loves in this way—but how delightful
it is! It has no title.

> Bright star! would I were steadfast as thou art—
>   Not in lone splendour hung aloft the night
> And watching, with eternal lids apart,
>   Like nature's patient, sleepless Eremite,
> The moving waters at their priest-like task
>   Of pure ablution round earth's human shores,
> Or gazing on new soft-fallen mask
>   Of snow upon the mountains and the moors—
>
> No—yet still steadfast, still unchangeable,
>   Pillow'd upon my fair love's ripening breast,
> To feel forever its soft fall and swell,
>   Awake forever in a sweet unrest,
> Still, still to hear her tender-taken breath,
> And so live ever—or else swoon to death.

Tennyson has charmingly represented a lover

wishing that he were a necklace of his beloved, or
her girdle, or her earring; but that is not a cosmic
emotion at all. Indeed, the idea of Tennyson's
pretty song was taken from old French and English love songs of the peasants—popular ballads.
But in this beautiful sonnet of Keats, where the
lover wishes to be endowed with the immortality
and likeness of a star only to be forever with the
beloved, there is something of the old Greek
thought which inspired the beautiful lines written
between two and three thousand years ago, and
translated by J. A. Symonds:

Gazing on stars, my Star? Would that I were the welkin,
Starry with myriad eyes, ever to gave upon thee!

But there is more than the Greek beauty of
thought in Keats's sonnet, for we find the poet
speaking of the exterior universe in the largest
relation, thinking of the stars watching forever
the rising and the falling of the sea tides, thinking
of the sea tides themselves as continually purify-
ing the world, even as a priest purifies a temple.
The fancy of the boy expands to the fancy of
philosophy; it is a blending of poetry, philosophy,
and sincere emotion.

You will have seen by the examples which we
have been reading together that English love
poetry, like Japanese love poetry, may be divided
into many branches and classified according to the
range of subject from the very simplest utterance

of feeling up to that highest class expressing cosmic emotion. Very rich the subject is; the student
is only puzzled where to choose. I should again
suggest to you to observe the value of the theme
of illusion, especially as illustrated in our examples. There are indeed multitudes of Western
love poems that would probably appear to you
very strange, perhaps very foolish. But you will
certainly acknowledge that there are some varieties of English love poetry which are neither
strange nor foolish, and which are well worth
studying, not only in themselves but in their relation to the higher forms of emotional expression
in all literature. Out of love poetry belonging to
the highest class, much can be drawn that would
serve to enrich and to give a new colour to your
own literature of emotion.

CHAPTER III

THE IDEAL WOMAN IN ENGLISH POETRY

As I gave already in this class a lecture on the subject of love poetry, you will easily understand that the subject of the present lecture is not exactly love. It is rather about love's imagining of perfect character and perfect beauty. The part of it to which I think your attention could be deservedly given is that relating to the imagined wife of the future, for this is a subject little treated of in Eastern poetry. It is a very pretty subject. But in Japan and other countries of the East almost every young man knows beforehand whom he is likely to marry. Marriage is arranged by the family: it is a family matter, indeed a family duty and not a romantic pursuit. At one time, very long ago, in Europe, marriages were arranged in much the same way. But nowadays it may be said in general that no young man in England or America can even imagine whom he will marry. He has to find his wife for himself; and he has nobody to help him; and if he makes a mistake, so much the worse for him. So to Western imagination the wife of the future is a mystery, a romance, an anxiety—something to dream about and to write poetry about.

This little book that I hold in my hand is now very rare. It is out of print, but it is worth mentioning to you because it is the composition of an exquisite man of letters, Frederick Locker-Lampson, best of all nineteenth century writers of society verse. It is called "Patchwork." Many years ago the author kept a kind of journal in which he wrote down or copied all the most beautiful or most curious things which he had heard or which he had found in books. Only the best things remained, so the value of the book is his taste in selection. Whatever Locker-Lampson pronounced good, the world now knows to have been exactly what he pronounced, for his taste was very fine. And in this book I find a little poem quoted from Mr. Edwin Arnold, now Sir Edwin. Sir Edwin Arnold is now old and blind, and he has not been thought of kindly enough in Japan, because his work has not been sufficiently known. Some people have even said his writings did harm to Japan, but I want to assure you that such statements are stupid lies. On the contrary he did for Japan whatever good the best of his talent as a poet and the best of his influence as a great journalist could enable him to do. But to come back to our subject: when Sir Edwin was a young student he had his dreams about marriage like other young English students, and he put one

of them into verse, and that verse was at once
picked out by Frederick Locker-Lampson for his
little book of gems. Half a century has passed
since then; but Locker-Lampson's judgment remains good, and I am going to put this little poem
first because it so well illustrates the subject of the
lecture. It is entitled "A Ma Future."

Where waitest thou,
   Lady, I am to love? Thou comest not,
   Thou knowest of my sad and lonely lot—
I looked for thee ere now!

It is the May,
   And each sweet sister soul hath found its brother,
   Only we two seek fondly each the other,
And seeking still delay.

Where art thou, sweet?
   I long for thee as thirsty lips for streams,
   O gentle promised angel of my dreams,
Why do we never meet?

Thou art as I,
   Thy soul doth wait for mine as mine for thee;
   We cannot live apart, must meeting be
Never before we die?

Dear Soul, not so,
   For time doth keep for us some happy years,
   And God hath portioned us our smiles and tears,
Thou knowest, and I know.

Therefore I bear
  This winter-tide as bravely as I may,
  Patiently waiting for the bright spring day
That cometh with thee, Dear.

'Tis the May light
  That crimsons all the quiet college gloom,
  May it shine softly in thy sleeping room,
And so, dear wife, good night!

This is, of course, addressed to the spirit of the unknown future wife. It is pretty, though it is only the work of a young student. But some one hundred years before, another student—a very great student, Richard Crashaw,—had a fancy of the same kind, and made verses about it which are famous. You will find parts of his poem about the imaginary wife in the ordinary anthologies, but not all of it, for it is very long. I will quote those verses which seem to me the best.

WISHES

Whoe'er she be,
That not impossible She,
That shall command my heart and me;

Where'er she lie,
Locked up from mortal eye,
In shady leaves of Destiny;

Till that ripe birth
Of studied Fate stand forth,
And teach her fair steps to our earth;

Till that divine
Idea take a shrine
Of crystal flesh, through which to shine;

Meet you her, my wishes,
Bespeak her to my blisses,
And be ye called my absent kisses.

The poet is supposing that the girl whom he is
to marry may not as yet even have been born, for
though men in the world of scholarship can marry
only late in life, the wife is generally quite young.
Marriage is far away in the future for the student, therefore these fancies. What he means to
say in short is about like this:

"Oh, my wishes, go out of my heart and look
for the being whom I am destined to marry—find
the soul of her, whether born or yet unborn, and
tell that soul of the love that is waiting for it."
Then he tries to describe the imagined woman he
hopes to find:

I wish her beauty
That owes not all its duty
To gaudy 'tire or glist'ring shoe-tie.

Something more than
Taffeta or tissue can;
Or rampant feather, or rich fan.

More than the spoil
Of shop or silk worm's toil,
Or a bought blush, or a set smile.

A face that's best
By its own beauty drest
And can alone command the rest.

A face made up
Out of no other shop
Than what nature's white hand sets ope.

A cheek where grows
More than a morning rose
Which to no box his being owes.

.   .   .   .   .

Eyes that displace
The neighbor diamond and outface
That sunshine by their own sweet grace.

Tresses that wear
Jewels, but to declare
How much themselves more precious are.

.   .   .   .   .

Smiles, that can warm
The blood, yet teach a charm
That chastity shall take no harm.

.   .   .   .   .

Life, that dares send
A challenge to his end,
And when it comes, say "Welcome, friend!"

There is much more, but the best of the
thoughts are here. They are not exactly new
thoughts, nor strange thoughts, but they are finely
expressed in a strong and simple way.

There is another composition on the same sub-

ject—the imaginary spouse, the destined one.
But this is written by a woman, Christina Rossetti.

SOMEWHERE OR OTHER

Somewhere or other there must surely be
    The face not seen, the voice not heard,
The heart that not yet—never yet—ah me!
    Made answer to my word.

Somewhere or other, may be near or far;
    Past land and sea, clean out of sight;
Beyond the wondering moon, beyond the star
    That tracks her night by night.

Somewhere or other, may be far or near;
    With just a wall, a hedge between;
With just the last leaves of the dying year,
    Fallen on a turf grown green.

And that turf means of course the turf of a
grave in the churchyard. This poem expresses
fear that the destined one never can be met, because death may come before the meeting time.
All through the poem there is the suggestion of
an old belief that for every man and for every
woman there must be a mate, yet that it is a chance
whether the mate will ever be found.

You observe that all of these are ghostly
poems, whether prospective or retrospective.
Here is another prospective poem:

AMATURUS

Somewhere beneath the sun,
   These quivering heart-strings prove it,
Somewhere there must be one
   Made for this soul, to move it;
Someone that hides her sweetness
   From neighbors whom she slights,
Nor can attain completeness,
   Nor give her heart its rights;
Someone whom I could court
   With no great change of manner,
Still holding reason's fort
   Though waving fancy's banner;
A lady, not so queenly
   As to disdain my hand,
Yet born to smile serenely
   Like those that rule the land;
Noble, but not too proud;
   With soft hair simply folded,
And bright face crescent-browed
   And throat by Muses moulded;

    .   .   .   .

Keen lips, that shape soft sayings
   Like crystals of the snow,
With pretty half-betrayings
   Of things one may not know;
Fair hand, whose touches thrill,
   Like golden rod of wonder,
Which Hermes wields at will
   Spirit and flesh to sunder.

    .   .   .   .

Forth, Love, and find this maid,
  Wherever she be hidden;
Speak, Love, be not afraid,
  But plead as thou art bidden;
And say, that he who taught thee
  His yearning want and pain,
Too dearly dearly bought thee
  To part with thee in vain.

These lines are by the author of that exquisite
little book "Ionica"—a book about which I hope
to talk to you in another lecture. His real name
was William Cory, and he was long the head-
master of an English public school, during which
time he composed and published anonymously the
charming verses which have made him famous—
modelling his best work in close imitation of the
Greek poets. A few expressions in these lines
need explanation. For instance, the allusion to
Hermes and his rod. I think you know that
Hermes is the Greek name of the same god whom
the Romans called Mercury,—commonly represented as a beautiful young man, naked and running quickly, having wings attached to the sandals
upon his feet. Runners used to pray to him for
skill in winning foot races. But this god had many
forms and many attributes, and one of his supposed duties was to bring the souls of the dead
into the presence of the king of Hades. So you
will see some pictures of him standing before the
throne of the king of the Dead, and behind him

a long procession of shuddering ghosts. He is
nearly always pictured as holding in his hands a
strange sceptre called the *caduceus,* a short staff
about which two little serpents are coiled, and at
the top of which is a tiny pair of wings. This is
the golden rod referred to by the poet; when
Hermes touched anybody with it, the soul of the
person touched was obliged immediately to leave
the body and follow after him. So it is a very
beautiful stroke of art in this poem to represent
the touch of the hand of great love as having the
magical power of the golden rod of Hermes. It
is as if the poet were to say: "Should she but
touch me, I know that my spirit would leap out of
my body and follow after her." Then there is
the expression "crescent-browed." It means only
having beautifully curved eyebrows—arched eyebrows being considered particularly beautiful in
Western countries.

Now we will consider another poem of the
ideal. What we have been reading referred to
ghostly ideals, to memories, or to hopes. Let us
now see how the poets have talked about realities.
Here is a pretty thing by Thomas Ashe. It is entitled "Pansie"; and this flower name is really a
corruption of a French word "Penser," meaning
a thought. The flower is very beautiful, and its
name is sometimes given to girls, as in the present
case.

MEET WE NO ANGELS, PANSIE?

Came, on a Sabbath noon, my sweet,
  In white, to find her lover;
The grass grew proud beneath her feet,
  The green elm-leaves above her:—
    Meet we no angels, Pansie?

She said, " We meet no angels now;"
  And soft lights stream'd upon her;
And with white hand she touch'd a bough;
  She did it that great honour:—
    What! meet no angels, Pansie?

O sweet brown hat, brown hair, brown eyes,
  Down-dropp'd brown eyes, so tender!
Then what said I? Gallant replies
  Seem flattery, and offend her:—
    But—meet no angels, Pansie?

The suggestion is obvious, that the maiden realizes to the lover's eye the ideal of an angel. As she comes he asks her slyly,—for she has been to the church—"Is it true that nobody ever sees real angels?" She answers innocently, thinking him to be in earnest, "No—long ago people used to see angels, but in these times no one ever sees them." He does not dare tell her how beautiful she seems to him; but he suggests much more than admiration by the tone of his protesting response to her answer: "What! You cannot mean to say that there are no angels now?" Of course that is the same as to say, "I see an angel now"—but the

girl is much too innocent to take the real and flat-
tering meaning.

Wordsworth's portrait of the ideal woman is
very famous; it was written about his own wife,
though that fact would not be guessed from the
poem. The last stanza is the most famous, but
we had better quote them all.

> She was a phantom of delight
> When first she gleamed upon my sight;
> A lovely apparition, sent
> To be a moment's ornament;
> Her eyes as stars of twilight fair;
> Like twilight's, too, her dusky hair;
> But all things else about her drawn
> From May-time and the cheerful dawn;
> A dancing shape, an image gay,
> To haunt, to startle, and waylay.
>
> I saw her upon nearer view,
> A Spirit, yet a Woman too!
> Her household motions light and free,
> And steps of virgin liberty;
> A countenance in which did meet
> Sweet records, promises as sweet;
> A creature not too bright or good
> For human nature's daily food;
> For transient sorrows, simple wiles,
> Praise, blame, love, kisses, tears and smiles.
>
> And now I see with eye serene
> The very pulse of the machine;
> A being breathing thoughtful breath,

A traveller betwixt life and death;
The reason firm, the temperate will,
Endurance, foresight, strength, and skill;
A perfect woman, nobly plann'd,
To warn, to comfort and command;
And yet a Spirit still, and bright
With something of angelic light.

I quoted this after the Pansie poem to show you how much more deeply Wordsworth could touch the same subject. To him, too, the first apparition of the ideal maiden seemed angelic; like Ashe he could perceive the mingled attraction of innocence and of youth. But innocence and youth are by no means all that make up the best attributes of woman; character is more than innocence and more than youth, and it is character that Wordsworth studies. But in the last verse he tells us that the angel is always there, nevertheless, even when the good woman becomes old. The angel is the Mother-soul.

Wordsworth's idea that character is the supreme charm was expressed very long before him by other English poets, notably by Thomas Carew.

He that loves a rosy cheek,
  Or a coral lip admires,
Or from star-like eyes doth seek
  Fuel to maintain his fires:
As old Time makes these decay,
  So his flames must waste away.

But a smooth and steadfast mind,
  Gentle thoughts and calm desires,
Hearts with equal love combined,
  Kindle never-dying fires.
Where these are not, I despise
Lovely cheeks or lips or eyes.

For about three hundred years in English literature it was the fashion—a fashion borrowed from the Latin poets—to speak of love as a fire or flame, and you must understand the image in these verses in that signification. To-day the fashion is not quite dead, but very few poets now follow it.

Byron himself, with all his passion and his affected scorn of ethical convention, could and did, when he pleased, draw beautiful portraits of moral as well as physical attraction. These stanzas are famous; they paint for us a person with equal attraction of body and mind.

She walks in beauty, like the night
  Of cloudless climes and starry skies;
And all that's best of dark and bright
  Meet in her aspect and her eyes:
Thus mellow'd to that tender light
  Which heaven to gaudy day denies.

One shade the more, one ray the less,
  Had half impair'd the nameless grace
Which waves in every raven tress,
  Or softly lightens o'er her face;

Where thoughts serenely sweet express
　How pure, how dear their dwelling-place.

And on that cheek, and o'er that brow,
　So soft, so calm, yet eloquent,
The smiles that win, the tints that glow,
　But tell of days in goodness spent,
A mind at peace with all below,
　A heart whose love is innocent!

It is worth noticing that in each of the last three poems, the physical beauty described is that of dark eyes and hair. This may serve to remind you that there are two distinct types, opposite types, of beauty celebrated by English poets; and the next poem which I am going to quote, the beautiful "Ruth" of Thomas Hood, also describes a dark woman.

She stood breast-high amid the corn,
Clasp'd by the golden light of morn,
Like the sweetheart of the sun,
Who many a glowing kiss had won.

On her cheek an autumn flush,
Deeply ripen'd;—such a blush
In the midst of brown was born,
Like red poppies grown with corn.

Round her eyes her tresses fell,
Which were blackest none could tell,
But long lashes veil'd a light,
That had else been all too bright.

And her hat, with shady brim,
Made her tressy forehead dim;
Thus she stood among the stooks,
Praising God with sweetest looks:—

Sure, I said, Heav'n did not mean,
Where I reap thou shouldst but glean,
Lay thy sheaf adown and come,
Share my harvest and my home.

We might call this the ideal of a peasant girl whose poverty appeals to the sympathy of all who behold her. The name of the poem is suggested indeed by the Bible story of Ruth the gleaner, but the story in the poem is only that of a rich farmer who marries a very poor girl, because of her beauty and her goodness. It is just a charming picture—a picture of the dark beauty which is so much admired in Northern countries, where it is less common than in Southern Europe. There are beautiful brown-skinned types; and the flush of youth on the cheeks of such a brown girl has been compared to the red upon a ripe peach or a russet apple—a hard kind of apple, very sweet and juicy, which is brown instead of yellow, or reddish brown. But the poet makes the comparison with poppy flowers and wheat. That, of course, means golden yellow and red; in English wheat fields red poppy flowers grow in abundance. The expression "tressy forehead" in the second line of the fourth stanza means a forehead half covered with falling, loose hair.

The foregoing pretty picture may be offset by a charming poem of Browning's describing a lover's pride in his illusion. It is simply entitled "Song," and to appreciate it you must try to understand the mood of a young man who believes that he has actually realized his ideal, and that the woman that he loves is the most beautiful person in the whole world. The fact that this is simply imagination on his part does not make the poem less beautiful—on the contrary, the false imagining is just what makes it beautiful, the youthful emotion of a moment being so humanly and frankly described. Such a youth must imagine that every one else sees and thinks about the girl just as he does, and he expects them to confess it.

> Nay but you, who do not love her,
>   Is she not pure gold, my mistress?
> Holds earth aught—speak truth—above her?
>   Aught like this tress, see, and this tress,
> And this last fairest tress of all,
> So fair, see, ere I let it fall?
>
> Because you spend your lives in praising;
>   To praise, you search the wide world over;
> Then why not witness, calmly gazing,
>   If earth holds aught—speak truth—above her?
> Above this tress, and this, I touch
> But cannot praise, I love so much!

You see the picture, I think,—probably some

artist's studio for a background. She sits or
stands there with her long hair loosely flowing
down to her feet like a river of gold; and her
lover, lifting up some of the long tresses in his
hand, asks his friend, who stands by, to notice how
beautiful such hair is. Perhaps the girl was having her picture painted. One would think so from
the question, "Since your business is to look
for beautiful things, why can you not honestly
acknowledge that this woman is the most beautiful
thing in the whole world?" Or we might imagine the questioned person to be a critic by profession as well as an artist. Like the preceding
poem this also is a picture. But the next poem,
also by Browning, is much more than a picture—
it is very profound indeed, simple as it looks. An
old man is sitting by the dead body of a young
girl of about sixteen. He tells us how he secretly
loved her, as a father might love a daughter, as
a brother might love a sister. But he would have
wished, if he had not been so old, and she so
young, to love her as a husband. He never could
have her in this world, but why should he not
hope for it in the future world? He whispers
into her dead ear his wish, and he puts a flower
into her dead hand, thinking, "When she wakes
up, in another life, she will see that flower, and
remember what I said to her, and how much I
loved her." That is the mere story. But we
must understand that the greatness of the love

expressed in the poem is awakened by an ideal of innocence and sweetness and goodness, and the affection is of the soul—that is to say, it is the love of beautiful character, not the love of a beautiful face only, that is expressed.

EVELYN HOPE

Beautiful Evelyn Hope is dead!
  Sit and watch by her side an hour.
That is her book-shelf, this her bed;
  She plucked that piece of geranium-flower,
Beginning to die too, in the glass;
  Little has yet been changed, I think:
The shutters are shut, no light can pass
  Save two long rays through the hinge's chink.

Sixteen years old when she died!
  Perhaps she had scarcely heard my name;
It was not her time to love; beside,
  Her life had many a hope and aim,
Duties enough and little cares,
  And now was quiet, now astir,
Till God's hand beckoned unawares,—
  And the sweet white brow is all of her.

Is it too late, then, Evelyn Hope?
  What, your soul was pure and true,
The good stars met in your horoscope,
  Made you of spirit, fire and dew—
And just because I was thrice as old
  And our paths in the world diverged so wide,
Each was naught to each, must I be told?
  We were fellow mortals, naught beside?

No, indeed! for God above,
  Is great to grant, as mighty to make,
And creates the love to reward the love:
  I claim you still, for my own love's sake!
Delayed it may be for more lives yet,
  Through worlds I shall traverse, not a few:
Much is to learn, much to forget,
  Ere the time be come for taking you.

But the time will come,—at last it will,
  When, Evelyn Hope, what meant (I shall say)
In the lower earth, in the years long still,
  That body and soul so pure and gay?
Why your hair was amber, I shall divine,
  And your mouth of your own geranium's red—
And what you would do with me, in fine,
  In the new life come in the old one's stead.

I have lived (I shall say) so much since then,
  Given up myself so many times,
Gained me the gains of various men,
  Ransacked the ages, spoiled the climes;
Yet one thing, one, in my soul's full scope,
  Either I missed or itself missed me:
And I want and find you, Evelyn Hope!
  What is the issue? let us see!

I loved you, Evelyn, all the while!
  My heart seemed full as it could hold;
There was space and to spare for the frank young smile,
  And the red young mouth, and the hair's young gold.
So, hush,—I will give you this leaf to keep:
  See, I shut it inside the sweet cold hand!

There, that is our secret: go to sleep!
You will wake, and remember, and understand.

No other poet has written so many different
kinds of poems on this subject as Browning; and
although I can not quote all of them, I must not
neglect to make a just representation of the variety. Here is another example: the chief idea
is again the beauty of truthfulness and fidelity,
but the artistic impression is quite different.

> A simple ring with a single stone,
>   To the vulgar eye no stone of price:
> Whisper the right word, that alone—
>   Forth starts a sprite, like fire from ice.
> And lo, you are lord (says an Eastern scroll)
> Of heaven and earth, lord whole and sole
>   Through the power in a pearl.
>
> A woman ('tis I this time that say)
>   With little the world counts worthy praise:
> Utter the true word—out and away
>   Escapes her soul; I am wrapt in blaze,
> Creation's lord, of heaven and earth
> Lord whole and sole—by a minute's birth—
>   Through the love in a girl!

Paraphrased, the meaning will not prove as
simple as the verses: Here is a finger ring set with
one small stone, one jewel. It is a very cheap-
looking stone to common eyes. But if you know
a certain magical word, and, after putting the
ring on your finger, you whisper that magical

word over the cheap-looking stone, suddenly a
spirit, a demon or a genie, springs from that gem
like a flash of fire miraculously issuing from a
lump of ice. And that spirit or genie has power to
make you king of the whole world and of the sky
above the world, lord of the spirits of heaven and
earth and air and fire. Yet the stone is only a
pearl—and it can make you lord of the universe.
That is the old Arabian story. The word scroll
here means a manuscript, an Arabian manuscript.

But what is after all the happiness of mere
power? There is a greater happiness possible
than to be lord of heaven and earth; that is the
happiness of being truly loved. Here is a woman;
to the eye of the world, to the sight of other men,
she is not very beautiful nor at all remarkable in
any way. She is just an ordinary woman, as the
pearl in the ring is to all appearances just a common pearl. But let the right word be said, let
the soul of that woman be once really touched by
the magic of love, and what a revelation! As the
spirit in the Arabian story sprang from the stone
of the magical ring, when the word was spoken,
so from the heart of this woman suddenly her
soul displays itself in shining light. And the man
who loves, instantly becomes, in the splendour of
that light, verily the lord of heaven and earth;
to the eyes of the being who loves him he is a god.

The legend is the legend of Solomon—not the
Solomon of the Bible, but the much more won-

derful Solomon of the Arabian story-teller. His power is said to have been in a certain seal ring, upon which the mystical name of Allah, or at least one of the ninety and nine mystical names, was engraved. When he chose to use this ring, all the spirits of air, the spirits of earth, the spirits of water and the spirits of fire were obliged to obey him. The name of such a ring is usually "Talisman."

Here is another of Browning's jewels, one of the last poems written shortly before his death. It is entitled "Summum Bonum,"—signifying "the highest good." The subject is a kiss; we may understand that the first betrothal kiss is the mark of affection described. When the promise of marriage has been made, that promise is sealed or confirmed by the first kiss. But this refers only to the refined classes of society. Among the English people proper, especially the country folk, kissing the girls is only a form of showing mere good will, and has no serious meaning at all.

All the breath and the bloom of the year in the bag of
    one bee:
  All the wonder and wealth of the mine in the heart of
    one gem:
In the core of one pearl all the shade and the shine of
    the sea:
  Breath and bloom, shade and shine,—wonder, wealth,
    and—how far above them—
Truth, that's brighter than gem,
  Trust, that's purer than pearl,—

Brightest truth, purest trust in the universe—all were
　　for me
In the kiss of one girl.

There is in this a suggestion of Ben Jonson,
who uses almost exactly the same simile without
any moral significance. The advantage of Browning is that he has used the sensuous imagery for
ethical symbolism; here he greatly surpasses Jonson, though it would be hard to improve upon the
beauty of Jonson's verses, as merely describing
visual beauty. Here are Jonson's stanzas:

THE TRIUMPH

See the Chariot at hand here of Love,
　　Wherein my Lady rideth!
Each that draws is a swan or a dove,
　　And well the car Love guideth.
As she goes, all hearts do duty
　　Unto her beauty;
And enamoured do wish, so they might
　　But enjoy such a sight,
That they still were to run by her side,
Through swords, through seas, whither she would ride.

Do but look on her eyes, they do light
　　All that Love's world compriseth!
Do but look on her hair, it is bright
　　As love's star when it riseth!
Do but mark, her forehead's smoother
　　Than words that soothe her;

And from her arch'd brows such a grace
  Sheds itself through the face,
As alone there triumphs to the life
All the gain, all the good, of the elements' strife.

Have you seen but a bright lily grow
  Before rude hands have touched it?
Have you mark'd but the fall of the snow
  Before the soil hath smutch'd it?
Have you felt the wool of beaver
  Or swan's down ever?
Or have smelt o' the bud o' the brier,
  Or the nard in the fire?
Or have tasted the bag of the bee?
O so white, O so soft, O so sweet is she!

The first of the above stanzas is a study after the Roman poets; but the last stanza is Jonson's own and is very famous. You will see that Browning was probably inspired by him, but I think that his verses are much more beautiful in thought and feeling.

There is one type of ideal woman very seldom described in poetry—the old maid, the woman whom sorrow or misfortune prevents from fulfilling her natural destiny. Commonly the woman who never marries is said to become cross, bad tempered, unpleasant in character. She could not be blamed for this, I think; but there are old maids who always remain as unselfish and frank and kind as a girl, and who keep the charm of girlhood even when their hair is white. Hartley

Coleridge, son of the great Samuel, attempted to describe such a one, and his picture is both touching and beautiful.

THE SOLITARY-HEARTED

She was a queen of noble Nature's crowning,
  A smile of hers was like an act of grace;
She had no winsome looks, no pretty frowning,
  Like daily beauties of the vulgar race:
But if she smiled, a light was on her face,
  A clear, cool kindliness, a lunar beam
Of peaceful radiance, silvering o'er the stream
  Of human thought with unabiding glory;
Not quite a waking truth, not quite a dream,
  A visitation, bright and transitory.

But she is changed,—hath felt the touch of sorrow,
  No love hath she, no understanding friend;
O grief! when Heaven is forced of earth to borrow
  What the poor niggard earth has not to lend;
But when the stalk is snapt, the rose must bend.
  The tallest flower that skyward rears its head
Grows from the common ground, and there must shed
  Its delicate petals. Cruel fate, too surely
That they should find so base a bridal bed,
  Who lived in virgin pride, so sweet and purely.

She had a brother, and a tender father,
  And she was loved, but not as others are
From whom we ask return of love,—but rather
  As one might love a dream; a phantom fair
Of something exquisitely strange and rare,
  Which all were glad to look on, men and maids,

Yet no one claimed—as oft, in dewy glades,
   The peering primrose, like a sudden gladness,
Gleams on the soul, yet unregarded fades;—
   The joy is ours, but all its own the sadness.

'Tis vain to say—her worst of grief is only
   The common lot, which all the world have known
To her 'tis more, because her heart is lonely,
   And yet she hath no strength to stand alone,—
Once she had playmates, fancies of her own,
   And she did love them. They are past away
As fairies vanish at the break of day;
   And like a spectre of an age departed,
Or unsphered angel woefully astray,
   She glides along—the solitary-hearted.

Perhaps it is scarcely possible for you to imagine that a woman finds it impossible to marry because of being too beautiful, too wise, and too good. In Western countries it is not impossible at all. You must try to imagine entirely different social conditions—conditions in which marriage depends much more upon the person than upon the parents, much more upon inclination than upon anything else. A woman's chances of marriage depend very much upon herself, upon her power of pleasing and charming. Thousands and tens of thousands can never get married. Now there are cases in which a woman can please too much. Men become afraid of her. They think, "She knows too much, I dare not be frank with her"—or, "She is too beautiful, she never would accept a common person like me"—or, "She is too formal and correct, she would never forgive a mistake, and I could never be happy with her." Not only is this possible, but it frequently happens. Too much excellence makes a misfortune. I think you can understand it best by the reference to the very natural prejudice against over-educated women, a prejudice founded upon experience and existing in all countries, even in Japan. Men are not attracted to a woman because she is excellent at mathematics, because she knows eight or nine different languages, because she has acquired all the conventions of high-pressure training. Men do not care about that. They want love and trust and kindliness and ability to make a home beautiful and happy. Well, the poem we have been reading is very pathetic because it describes a woman who can not fulfil her natural destiny, can not be loved—this through no fault of her own, but quite the reverse. To be too much advanced beyond one's time and environment is even a worse misfortune than to be too much behind.

CHAPTER IV

PERHAPS there is an idea among Japanese students that one general difference between Japanese and Western poetry is that the former cul-
tivates short forms and the latter longer ones.
But this is only in part true. It is true that short
forms of poetry have been cultivated in the Far
East more than in modern Europe; but in all
European literature short forms of poetry are to
be found—indeed quite as short as anything in
Japanese. Like the Japanese, the old Greeks,
who carried poetry to the highest perfection that
it has ever attained, delighted in short forms; and
the Greek Anthology is full of compositions containing only two or three lines. You will find
beautiful translations of these in Symonds's "Studies of Greek Poets," in the second volume. Following Greek taste, the Roman poets afterwards
cultivated short forms of verse, but they chiefly
used such verse for satirical purposes, unfortunately; I say, unfortunately, because the first great
English poets who imitated the ancients were
chiefly influenced by the Latin writers, and they

also used the short forms for epigrammatic satire, rarely for a purely esthetic object. Ben Jonson both wrote and translated a great number of very short stanzas—two lines and four lines; but Jonson was a satirist in these forms. Herrick, as you know, delighted in very short poems; but he was greatly influenced by Jonson, and many of his couplets and of his quatrains are worthless satires or worthless jests. However, you will find some short verses in Herrick that almost make you think of a certain class of Japanese poems. After the Elizabethan Age, also, the miniature poems were still used in the fashion set by the Roman writers,—then the eighteenth century deluged us with ill-natured witty epigrams of the like brief form. It was not until comparatively modern times that our Western world fully recognized the value of the distich, triplet or quatrain for the expression of beautiful thoughts, rather than for the expression of ill-natured ones. But now that the recognition has come, it has been discovered that nothing is harder than to write a beautiful poem of two or four lines. Only great masters have been truly successful at it. Goethe, you know, made a quatrain that has become a part of world-literature:

> Who ne'er his bread in sorrow ate,—
> Who ne'er the lonely midnight hours,
> Weeping upon his bed has sate,
> He knows ye not, ye Heavenly Powers!

—meaning, of course, that inspiration and wisdom come to us only through sorrow, and that those who have never suffered never can be wise. But in the universities of England a great deal of short work of a most excellent kind has been done in Greek and Latin; and there is the celebrated case of an English student who won a prize by a poem of a single line. The subject given had been the miracle of Christ's turning water into wine at the marriage feast; and while other scholars attempted elaborate composition on the theme, this student wrote but one verse, of which the English translation is

The modest water saw its Lord, and blushed.

Of course the force of the idea depends upon the popular conception of wine being red. The Latin and Greek model, however, did not seem to encourage much esthetic effort in short poems of English verse ·until the time of the romantic movement. Then, both in France and England, many brief forms of poetry made their appearance. In France, Victor Hugo attempted composition in astonishingly varied forms of verse— some forms actually consisting of only two syllables to a line. With this surprisingly short measure begins one of Hugo's most remarkably early poems, "Les Djins," representing the coming of evil spirits with a storm, their passing over the house where a man is at prayer, and departing into the distance again. Beginning with only two syllables to the line, the measure of the poem gradually widens as the spirits approach, becomes very wide, very long and sonorous as they reach the house, and again shrinks back to lines of two syllables as the sound of them dies away. In England a like variety of experiments has been made; but neither in France nor in England has the short form yet been as successfully cultivated as it was among the Greeks. We have some fine examples; but, as an eminent English editor observed a few years ago, not enough examples to make a book. And of course this means that there are very few; for you can make a book of poetry very well with as little as fifty pages of largely and widely printed text. However, we may cite a few modern instances.

I think that about the most perfect quatrains we have are those of the extraordinary man, Walter Savage Landor, who, you know, was a rare Greek scholar, all his splendid English work being very closely based upon the Greek models. He made a little epitaph upon himself, which is matchless of its kind:

I strove with none, for none was worth my strife;
  Nature I loved, and next to Nature, Art;
I warmed both hands before the fire of life:
  It sinks; and I am ready to depart.

You know that Greeks used the short form a

great deal for their exquisite epitaphs, and that a considerable part of the anthology consists of epitaphic literature. But the quatrain has a much wider range than this funereal limitation, and one such example of epitaph will suffice.

Only one English poet of our own day, and that a minor one, has attempted to make the poem of four lines a specialty—that is William Watson. He has written a whole volume of such little poems, but very few of them are successful. As I said before, we have not enough good poems of this sort for a book; and the reason is not because English poets despise the short form, but because it is supremely difficult. The Greeks succeeded in it, but we are still far behind the Greeks in the shaping of any kind of verse. The best of Watson's pieces take the form of philosophical suggestions; and this kind of verse is particularly well adapted to philosophical utterance.

> Think not thy wisdom can illume away
> The ancient tanglement of night and day.
> Enough to acknowledge both, and both revere;
> They see not clearliest who see all things clear.

That is to say, do not think that any human knowledge will ever be able to make you understand the mystery of the universe with its darkness and light, its joy and pain. It is best to revere the powers that make both good and evil, and to remember that the keenest, worldly, practical minds

are not the minds that best perceive the great
truths and mysteries of existence. Here is another little bit, reminding us somewhat of Goethe's
quatrain, already quoted.

Lives there whom pain hath evermore passed by
And sorrow shunned with an averted eye?
Him do thou pity,—him above the rest,
Him, of all hapless mortals most unblessed.

That needs no commentary, and it contains a
large truth in small space. Here is a little bit on
the subject of the artist's ambition, which is also
good.

The thousand painful steps at last are trod,
At last the temple's difficult door we win,
But perfect on his pedestal, the God
Freezes us hopeless when we enter in.

The higher that the artist climbs by effort, the
nearer his approach to the loftier truth, the more
he understands how little his very best can achieve.
It is the greatest artist, he who veritably enters
the presence of God—that most feels his own
weakness; the perception of beauty that other men
can not see, terrifies him, freezes him motionless,
as the poet says.

Out of all of Watson's epigrams I believe these
are the best. The rest with the possible exception
of those on the subject of love seem to me altogether failures. Emerson and various American

poets also attempted the quatrain—but Emerson's
verse is nearly always bad, even when his thought
is sublime.   One example of Emerson will suffice.

> Thou canst not wave thy staff in air,
>   Or dip thy paddle in the lake,
> But it carves the bow of beauty there,
>   And the ripples in rhyme the oar forsake.

The form is atrociously bad; but the reflection
is grand—it is another way of expressing the beautiful old Greek thought that "God *geometrizes*
everywhere"—that is, that all motion is in geo-
metrical lines, and full of beauty.   You can pick
hundreds of fine things in very short verse out of
Emerson, but the verse is nearly always shapeless;
the composition of the man invariably makes us
think of diamonds in the rough, jewels uncut.   So
far as form goes a much better master of quatrain
is the American poet Aldrich, who wrote the following little thing, entitled "Popularity."

> Such kings of shreds have wooed and won her,
>   Such crafty knaves her laurel owned,
> It has become almost an honour
>   Not to be crowned.

This is good verse.   The reference to "a king
of shreds and patches"—that is, a beggar king—
you will recognize as Shakespearean.   But although this pretty verse has in it more philosophy
than satire, it approaches the satiric class of epi-

grams. Neither America nor England has been able to do very much in the sort of verse that we have been talking about. Now this is a very remarkable thing,—because at the English universities beautiful work has been done in Greek or Latin—in poems of a single line, of two lines, of three lines and other very brief measures. Why can it not be done in English? I suspect that it is because our English language has not yet become sufficiently perfect, sufficiently flexible, sufficiently melodious to allow of great effect with a very few words. We can do the thing in Greek or in Latin because either Greek or Latin is a more perfect language.

So much for theory. I should like to suggest, however, that it is very probable many attempts at these difficult forms of poetry will be attempted by English poets within the next few years. There is now a tendency in that direction. I do not know whether such attempts will be successful; but I should like you to understand that for Western poets they are extremely difficult and that you ought to obtain from the recognition of this fact a new sense of the real value of your own short forms of verse in the hands of a master. Effects can be produced in Japanese which the Greeks could produce with few syllables, but which the English can not. Now it strikes me that, instead of even thinking of throwing away old forms of verse in order to invent new ones, the future Japanese poets ought rather to develop and cultivate and prize the forms already existing, which belong to the genius of the language, and which have proved themselves capable of much that no English verse or even French verse could accomplish. Perhaps only the Italian is really comparable to Japanese in some respects; you can perform miracles with Italian verse.

CHAPTER V

THE Western poet and writer of romance has exactly the same kind of difficulty in comprehending Eastern subjects as you have in comprehending Western subjects. You will commonly find references to Japanese love poems of the popular kind made in such a way as to indicate the writer's belief that such poems refer to married life or at least to a courtship relation. No Western writer who has not lived for many years in the East, could write correctly about anything on this subject; and even after a long stay in the country he might be unable to understand. Therefore a great deal of Western poetry written about Japan must seem to you all wrong, and I can not hope to offer you many specimens of work in this direction that could deserve your praise. Yet there is some poetry so fine on the subject of Japan that I think you would admire it and I am sure that you should know it. A proof of really great art is that it is generally true—it seldom falls into the misapprehensions to which minor art is liable. What do you think of the fact that the finest poetry ever written upon a Japanese subject by any Western poet, has been written by a man who never saw

86

the land? But he is a member of the French
Academy, a great and true lover of art, and without a living superior in that most difficult form of
poetry, the sonnet. In the time of thirty years he
produced only one very small volume of sonnets,
but so fine are these that they were lifted to the
very highest place in poetical distinction. I may
say that there are now only three really great
French poets—survivals of the grand romantic
school. These are Leconte de Lisle, Sully-Prud-
homme, and José Maria de Heredia. It is the last
of whom I am speaking. As you can tell by his
name, he is not a Frenchman either by birth or
blood, but a Spaniard, or rather a Spanish Creole,
born in Cuba. Heredia knows Japan only through
pictures, armour, objects of art in museums, paint-
ings and carvings. Remembering this, I think
that you will find that he does wonderfully well.
It is true that he puts a woman in one of his pictures, but I think that his management of his subject is very much nearer the truth than that of
almost any writer who has attempted to describe
old Japan. And you must understand that the
following sonnet is essentially intended to be a
picture—to produce upon the mind exactly the
same effect that a picture does, with the addition
of such life as poetry can give.

LE SAMOURAI

D'un doigt distrait frôlant la sonore bîva,
A travers les bambous tressés en fine latte,

Elle a vu, par la plage éblouissante et plate,
S'avancer le vainqueur que son amour rêva.

C'est lui. Sabres au flanc, l'éventail haut, il va.
La cordelière rouge et le gland écarlate
Coupent l'armure sombre, et, sur l'épaule, éclate
Le blazon de Hizen ou de Tokungawa.

Ce beau guerrier vêtu de lames et de plaques,
Sous le bronze, la soie et les brillantes laques,
Semble un crustacé noir, gigantesque et vermeil.

Il l'a vue. Il sourit dans la barbe du masque,
Et son pas plus hâtif fait reluire au soleil
Les deux antennes d'or qui tremblent à son casque.

"Lightly touching her *biva* with heedless finger,
she has perceived, through the finely woven bamboo
screen, the conqueror, lovingly thought of,
approach over the dazzling level of the beach.

"It is he. With his swords at his side he advances,
holding up his fan. The red girdle and
the scarlet tassel appear in sharply cut relief
against the dark armour; and upon his shoulder
glitters a crest of Hizen or of Tokungawa.

"This handsome warrior sheathed with his
scales and plates of metal, under his bronze, his
silk and glimmering lacquer, seems a crustacean,
gigantic, black and vermilion.

"He has caught sight of her. Under the beaver
of the war mask he smiles, and his quickened step

makes to glitter in the sun the two antennæ of gold that quiver upon his helmet."

The comparison of a warrior in full armour to a gigantic crab or lobster, especially lobster, is not exactly new. Victor Hugo has used it before in French literature, just as Carlyle has used it in English literature; indeed the image could not fail to occur to the artist in any country where the study of armour has been carried on. But here the poet does not speak of any particular creature; he uses only the generic term, crustacean, the vagueness of which makes the comparison much more effective. I think you can see the whole picture at once. It is a Japanese colour-print,—some ancient interior, lighted by the sun of a great summer day; and a woman looking through a bamboo blind toward the seashore, where she sees a warrior approaching. He divines that he is seen; but if he smiles, it is only because the smile is hidden by his iron mask. The only sign of any sentiment on his part is that he walks a little quicker. Still more amazing is a companion picture, containing only a solitary figure:

LE DAIMIO (Matin de bataille)
Sous le noir fouet de guerre à quadruple pompon,
L'étalon belliqueux en hennissant se cabre,
Et fait bruire, avec de cliquetis de sabre,
La cuirasse de bronze aux lames du jupon.

Le Chef vêtu d'airain, de laque et de crépon,
Otant le masque à poils de son visage glabre,
Regarde le volcan sur un ciel de cinabre
Dresser la neige où rit l'aurore du Nippon.

Mais il a vu, vers l'Est éclaboussé d'or, l'astre,
Glorieux d'éclairer ce matin de désastre,
Poindre, orbe éblouissant, au-dessus de la mer;

Et pour couvrir ses yeux dont pas un cil ne bouge,
Il ouvre d'un seul coup son éventail de fer,
Où dans le satin blanc se lève un Soleil rouge.

"Under the black war whip with its quadruple pompon the fierce stallion, whinnying, curvets, and makes the rider's bronze cuirass ring against the plates of his shirt of mail, with a sound like the clashing of sword blades.

"The Chief, clad in bronze and lacquer and silken crape, removing the bearded masque from his beardless face, turns his gaze to the great volcano, lifting its snows into the cinnabar sky where the dawn of Nippon begins to smile.

"Nay! he has already seen the gold-spattered day star, gloriously illuminating the morning of disaster, rise, a blinding disk, above the seas. And to shade his eyes, on both of which not even a single eyelash stirs, he opens with one quick movement his iron fan, wherein upon a field of white satin there rises a crimson sun."

Of course this hasty translation is very poor; and you can only get from it the signification and colour of the picture—the beautiful sonority and luminosity of the French is all gone. Nevertheless, I am sure that the more you study the original the more you will see how fine it is. Here also is a Japanese colour print. We see the figure of the horseman on the shore, in the light of dawn; behind him the still dark sky of night; before him the crimson dawn, and Fuji white against the red sky. And in the open fan, with its red sun, we have a grim suggestion of the day of blood that is about to be; that is all. But whoever reads that sonnet will never forget it; it burns into the memory. So, indeed, does everything that Heredia writes. Unfortunately he has not yet written anything more about Japan.

I have quoted Heredia because I think that no other poet has even approached him in the attempt to make a Japanese picture—though many others have tried; and the French, nearly always, have done much better than the English, because they are more naturally artists. Indeed one must be something of an artist to write anything in the way of good poetry on a Japanese subject. If you look at the collection "Poems of Places," in the library, you will see how poorly Japan is there represented; the only respectable piece of foreign work being by Longfellow, and that is only about Japanese vases. But since then some English poems have appeared which are at least worthy of Japanese notice.

CHAPTER VI

THE BIBLE IN ENGLISH LITERATURE

IT IS no exaggeration to say that the English Bible is, next to Shakespeare, the greatest work in English literature, and that it will have much more influence than even Shakespeare upon the written and spoken language of the English race. For this reason, to study English literature without some general knowledge of the relation of the Bible to that literature would be to leave one's literary education very incomplete. It is not necessary to consider the work from a religious point of view at all; indeed, to so consider it would be rather a hindrance to the understanding of its literary excellence. Some persons have ventured to say that it is only since Englishmen ceased to believe in the Bible that they began to discover how beautiful it was. This is not altogether true; but it is partly true. For it is one thing to consider every word of a book as the word of God or gods, and another thing to consider it simply as the work of men like ourselves. Naturally we should think it our duty to suppose the work of a divine being perfect in itself, and to imagine beauty and truth where neither really exists. The wonder of

the English Bible can really be best appreciated
by those who, knowing it to be the work of men
much less educated and cultivated than the scholars of the nineteenth century, nevertheless perceive that those men were able to do in literature
what no man of our own day could possibly do.
Of course in considering the work of the translators, we must remember the magnificence of the
original. I should not like to say that the Bible
is the greatest of all religious books. From the
moral point of view it contains very much that
we can not to-day approve of; and what is good
in it can be found in the sacred books of other nations. Its ethics can not even claim to be absolutely original. The ancient Egyptian scriptures
contain beauties almost superior in moral exaltation to anything contained in the Old Testament;
and the sacred books of other Eastern nations,
notably the sacred books of India, surpass the
Hebrew scriptures in the highest qualities of imagination and of profound thought. It is only of
late years that Europe, through the labour
of Sanskrit and Pali scholars, has become acquainted with the astonishing beauty of thought
and feeling which Indian scholars enshrined in
scriptures much more voluminous than the Hebrew Bible; and it is not impossible that this far-
off literature will some day influence European
thought quite as much as the Jewish Bible. Everywhere to-day in Europe and America the study of

Buddhist and Sanskrit literature is being pursued
not only with eagerness but with enthusiasm—an
enthusiasm which sometimes reaches to curious
extremes. I might mention, in example, the case
of a rich man who recently visited Japan on his
way from India. He had in New Zealand a valuable property; he was a man of high culture, and
of considerable social influence. One day he happened to read an English translation of the
"Bhagavad-Gita." Almost immediately he re-
solved to devote the rest of his life to religious
study in India, in a monastery among the mountains; and he gave up wealth, friends, society,
everything that Western civilization could offer
him, in order to seek truth in a strange country.
Certainly this is not the only instance of the kind;
and while such incidents can happen, we may feel
sure that the influence of religious literature is
not likely to die for centuries to come.

But every great scripture, whether Hebrew,
Indian, Persian, or Chinese, apart from its religious value will be found to have some rare and
special beauty of its own; and in this respect the
original Bible stands very high as a monument
of sublime poetry and of artistic prose. If it is
not the greatest of religious books as a literary
creation, it is at all events one of the greatest; and
the proof is to be found in the inspiration which
millions and hundreds of millions, dead and living,
have obtained from its utterances. The Semitic

races have always possessed in a very high degree
the genius of poetry, especially poetry in which
imagination plays a great part; and the Bible is
the monument of Semitic genius in this regard.
Something in the serious, stern, and reverential
spirit of the genius referred to made a particular
appeal to Western races having certain characteristics of the same kind. Themselves uncultivated
in the time that the Bible was first made known
to them, they found in it almost everything that
they thought and felt, expressed in a much better
way than they could have expressed it. Accordingly the Northern races of Europe found their
inspiration in the Bible; and the enthusiasm for it
has not yet quite faded away.

But the value of the original, be it observed, did
not make the value of the English Bible. Certainly it was an inspiring force; but it was nothing more. The English Bible is perhaps a much
greater piece of fine literature, altogether considered, than the Hebrew Bible. It was so for a particular reason which it is very necessary for the
student to understand. The English Bible is a
product of literary evolution.

In studying English criticisms upon different
authors, I think that you must have sometimes felt
impatient with the critics who told you, for example, that Tennyson was partly inspired by
Wordsworth and partly by Keats and partly by
Coleridge; and that Coleridge was partly inspired

by Blake and Blake by the Elizabethans, and so on. You may have been tempted to say, as I used very often myself to say, "What does it matter where the man got his ideas from? I care only for the beauty that is in his work, not for a history of his literary education." But to-day the value of the study of such relations appears in quite a new light. Evolutional philosophy, applied to the study of literature as to everything else, has shown us conclusively that man is not a god who can make something out of nothing, and that every great work of genius must depend even less upon the man of genius himself than upon the labours of those who lived before him. Every great author must draw his thoughts and his knowledge in part from other great authors, and these again from previous authors, and so on back, till we come to that far time in which there was no written literature, but only verses learned by heart and memorized by all the people of some one tribe or place, and taught by them to their children and to their grandchildren. It is only in Greek mythology that the divinity of Wisdom leaps out of a god's head, in full armour. In the world of reality the more beautiful a work of art, the longer, we may be sure, was the time required to make it, and the greater the number of different minds which assisted in its development.

So with the English Bible. No one man could have made the translation of 1611. No one generation of men could have done it. It was not the labour of a single century. It represented the work of hundreds of translators working through hundreds of years, each succeeding generation improving a little upon the work of the previous generation, until in the seventeenth century the best had been done of which the English brain and the English language was capable. In no other way can the surprising beauties of style and expression be explained. No subsequent effort could improve the Bible of King James. Every attempt made since the seventeenth century has only resulted in spoiling and deforming the strength and the beauty of the authorized text.

Now you will understand why, from the purely literary point of view, the English Bible is of the utmost importance for study. Suppose we glance for a moment at the principal events in the history of this evolution.

The first translation of the Bible into a Western tongue was that made by Jerome (commonly called Saint Jerome) in the fourth century; he translated directly from the Hebrew and other Arabic languages into Latin, then the language of the Empire. This translation into Latin was called the Vulgate,—from *vulgare*, "to make generally known." The Vulgate is still used in the Roman church. The first English translations which have been preserved to us were made from the Vulgate, not from the original tongues.

First of all, John Wycliffe's Bible may be called
the foundation of the seventeenth century Bible.
Wycliffe's translation, in which he was helped by
many others, was published between 1380 and
1388. So we may say that the foundation of the
English Bible dates from the fourteenth century,
one thousand years after Jerome's Latin translation. But Wycliffe's version, excellent as it was,
could not serve very long: the English language
was changing too quickly. Accordingly, in the
time of Henry VIII Tyndale and Coverdale, with
many others, made a new translation, this time
not from the Vulgate, but from the Greek text of
the great scholar Erasmus. This was the most
important literary event of the time, for "it coloured the entire complexion of subsequent English
prose,"—to use the words of Professor Gosse.
This means that all prose in English written since
Henry VIII has been influenced, directly or indirectly, by the prose of Tyndale's Bible, which
was completed about 1535. Almost at the same
time a number of English divines, under the super-
intendence of Archbishop Cranmer, gave to the
English language a literary treasure scarcely inferior to the Bible itself, and containing wonderful translations from the Scriptures,—the "Book
of Common Prayer." No English surpasses the
English of this book, still used by the Church; and
many translators have since found new inspiration
from it.

A revision of this famous Bible was made in 1565, entitled "The Bishops' Bible." The cause of the revision was largely doctrinal, and we need not trouble ourselves about this translation farther than to remark that Protestantism was re-shaping the Scriptures to suit the new state religion. Perhaps this edition may have had something to do with the determination of the Roman Catholics to make an English Bible of their own. The Jesuits began the work in 1582 at Rheims, and by 1610 the Roman Catholic version known as the Douay (or Douai) version—because of its having been made chiefly at the Catholic College of Douai in France—was completed. This version has many merits; next to the wonderful King James version, it is certainly the most poetical; and it has the further advantage of including a number of books which Protestantism has thrown out of the authorized version, but which have been used in the Roman church since its foundation. But I am speaking of the book only as a literary English production. It was not made with the help of original sources; its merits are simply those of a melodious translation from the Latin Vulgate.

At last, in 1611, was made, under the auspices of King James, the famous King James version; and this is the great literary monument of the English language. It was the work of many learned men; but the chief worker and supervisor was the Bishop of Winchester, Lancelot Andrews, perhaps the most eloquent English preacher that ever lived. He was a natural-born orator, with an exquisite ear for the cadences of language. To this natural faculty of the Bishop's can be attributed much of the musical charm of the English in which the Bible was written. Still, it must not be supposed that he himself did all the work, or even more than a small proportion of it. What he did was to tone it; he overlooked and corrected all the text submitted to him, and suffered only the best forms to survive. Yet what magnificent material he had to choose from! All the translations of the Bible that had been made before his time were carefully studied with a view to the conservation of the best phrases, both for sound and for form. We must consider the result not merely as a study of literature in itself, but also as a study of eloquence; for every attention was given to those effects to be expected from an oratorical recitation of the text in public.

This marks the end of the literary evolution of the Bible. Everything that has since been done has only been in the direction of retrogression, of injury to the text. We have now a great many later versions, much more scholarly, so far as correct scholarship is concerned, than the King James version, but none having any claim to literary importance. Unfortunately, exact scholars are

very seldom men of literary ability; the two faculties are rarely united. The Bible of 1870,
known as the Oxford Bible, and now used in the
Anglican state-church, evoked a great protest
from the true men of letters, the poets and critics
who had found their inspirations in the useful
study of the old version. The new version was
the work of fourteen years; it was made by the
united labour of the greatest scholars in the Eng-
lish-speaking world; and it is far the most exact
translation that we have. Nevertheless the literary quality has been injured to such an extent that
no one will ever turn to the new revision for poetical study. Even among the churches there was
a decided condemnation of this scholarly treatment of the old text; and many of the churches
refused to use the book. In this case, conserv-
atism is doing the literary world a service, keeping the old King James version in circulation,
and insisting especially upon its use in Sunday
schools.

We may now take a few examples of the differences between the revised version and the Bible
of King James. Professor Saintsbury, in an essay
upon English prose, published some years ago,
said that the most perfect piece of English prose
in the language was that comprised in the sixth
and seventh verses of the eighth chapter of the
Song of Songs:

Set me as a seal upon thine heart, as a seal upon thine arm: for love is strong as death; jealousy is cruel as the grave; the coals thereof are coals of fire, which hath a most vehement flame.

Many waters can not quench love, neither can the floods drown it: if a man would give all the substance of his house for love, it would utterly be condemned.

I should not like to say that the Professor is certainly right in calling this the finest prose in the English language; but he is a very great critic, whose opinion must be respected and considered, and the passage is certainly very fine. But in the revised version, how tame the same text has become in the hands of the scholarly translators!

The flashes thereof are flashes of fire, a very flame of the Lord.

Now as a description of jealousy, not to speak of the literary execution at all, which is the best? What, we may ask, has been gained by calling jealousy "a flame of the Lord" or by substituting the word "flashes" for "coals of fire"? All through the new version are things of this kind. For example, in the same Song of Songs there is a beautiful description of eyes, like "doves by the rivers of waters, washed with milk, and fitly set." By substituting "rivers" only for "rivers of waters" the text may have gained in exactness, but it has lost immeasurably, both in poetry and in sound. Far more poetical is the verse as given in the Douai version: "His eyes are as doves upon brooks of waters, which are washed with milk, and sit beside the beautiful streams."

It may even be said without any question that the mistakes of the old translators were often much more beautiful than the original. A splendid example is given in the verse of Job, chapter twenty-six, verse thirteen: "By his spirit he hath garnished the heavens; his hand hath formed the crooked serpent." By the crooked serpent was supposed to be signified the grand constellation called *Draco,* or the Dragon. And the figure is sublime. It is still more sublime in the Douai translation. "His obstetric hand hath brought forth the Winding Serpent." This is certainly a grand imagination—the hand of God, like the hand of a midwife, bringing forth a constellation out of the womb of the eternal night. But in the revised version, which is exact, we have only "His hand hath pierced the Swift Serpent!" All the poetry is dead.

There are two methods for the literary study of any book—the first being the study of its thought and emotion; the second only that of its workmanship. A student of literature should study some of the Bible from both points of view. In attempting the former method he will do well to consider many works of criticism, but for the study of the text as literature, his duty is very plain —the King James version is the only one that ought to form the basis of his study, though he

should look at the Douai version occasionally. Also
he should have a book of references, such as Cru-
den's Concordance, by help of which he can collect
together in a few moments all the texts upon any
particular subject, such as the sea, the wind, the
sky, human life, the shadows of evening. The
study of the Bible is not one which I should recommend to very young Japanese students, because
of the quaintness of the English. Before a good
knowledge of English forms is obtained, the
archaisms are apt to affect the students' mode of
expression. But for the advanced student of literature, I should say that some knowledge of the
finest books in the Bible is simply indispensable.
The important books to read are not many. But
one should read at least the books of Genesis,
Exodus, Ruth, Esther, the Song of Songs, Proverbs,—and, above all, Job. Job is certainly the
grandest book in the Bible; but all of those which
I have named are books that have inspired poets
and writers in all departments of English literature to such an extent that you can scarcely read a
masterpiece in which there is not some conscious
or unconscious reference to them. Another book
of philosophical importance is Ecclesiastes, where,
in addition to much proverbial wisdom, you will
find some admirable world-poetry—that is, poetry which contains universal truth about human
life in all times and all ages. Of the historical
books and the law books I do not think that it is

important to read much; the literary element in these is not so pronounced. It is otherwise with the prophetic books, but here in order to obtain a few jewels of expression, you have to read a great deal that is of little value. Of the New Testament there is very little equal to the Old in literary value; indeed, I should recommend the reading only of the closing book—the book called the Revelation, or the Apocalypse, from which we have derived a literary adjective "apocalyptic," to describe something at once very terrible and very grand. Whether one understands the meaning of this mysterious text makes very little difference; the sonority and the beauty of its sentences, together with the tremendous character of its imagery, can not but powerfully influence mind and ear, and thus stimulate literary taste. At least two of the great prose writers of the nineteenth century, Carlyle and Ruskin, have been vividly influenced by the book of the Revelation. Every period of English literature shows some influence of Bible study, even from the old Anglo-Saxon days; and during the present year, the study has so little slackened that one constantly sees announcements of new works upon the literary elements of the Bible. Perhaps one of the best is Professor Moulton's "Modern Reader's Bible," in which the literary side of the subject receives better consideration than in any other work of the kind published for general use.

CHAPTER VII

THE "HAVAMAL"

OLD NORTHERN ETHICS OF LIFE

Then from his lips in music rolled
The Havamal of Odin old,
With sounds mysterious as the roar
Of billows on a distant shore.

PERHAPS many of you who read this little verse
in Longfellow's "Saga of King Olaf" have wished
to know what was this wonderful song that the
ghost of the god sang to the king. I am afraid
that you would be very disappointed in some
respects by the "Havamal." There is indeed a
magical song in it; and it is this magical
song especially that Longfellow refers to, a
song of charms. But most of the "Havamal"
is a collection of ethical teaching. All that has
been preserved by it has been published and translated by Professors Vigfusson and Powell. It is
very old—perhaps the oldest Northern literature
that we have. I am going to attempt a short lecture upon it, because it is very closely related to
the subject of Northern character, and will help
us, perhaps better than almost anything else, to
understand how the ancestors of the English felt

and thought before they became Christians. Nor is this all. I venture to say that the character of the modern English people still retains much more of the quality indicated by the "Havamal" than of the quality implied by Christianity. The old Northern gods are not dead; they rule a very great part of the world to-day.

The proverbial philosophy of a people helps us to understand more about them than any other kind of literature. And this sort of literature is certainly among the oldest. It represents only the result of human experience in society, the wisdom that men get by contact with each other, the results of familiarity with right and wrong. By studying the proverbs of a people, you can always make a very good guess as to whether you could live comfortably among them or not.

Froude, in one of his sketches of travel in Norway, made the excellent observation that if we could suddenly go back to the time of the terrible sea-kings, if we could revisit to-day the homes of the old Northern pirates, and find them exactly as they were one thousand or fifteen hundred years ago, we should find them very much like the modern Englishmen—big, simple, silent men, concealing a great deal of shrewdness under an aspect of simplicity. The teachings of the "Havamal" give great force to this supposition. The book must have been known in some form to the early English—or at least the verses composing it (it is all written in verse) ; and as I have already said, the morals of the old English, as well as their character, differed very little from those of the men of the still further North, with whom they mingled and intermarried freely, both before and after the Danish conquest, when for one moment England and Sweden were one kingdom.

Of course you must remember that Northern society was a very terrible thing in some ways. Every man carried his life in his hands; every farmer kept sword and spear at his side even in his own fields; and every man expected to die fighting. In fact, among the men of the more savage North—the men of Norway in especial—it was considered a great disgrace to die of sickness, to die on one's bed. That was not to die like a man. Men would go out and get themselves killed, when they felt old age or sickness coming on. But these facts must not blind us to the other fact that there was even in that society a great force of moral cohesion, and sound principles of morality. If there had not been, it could not have existed; much less could the people who lived under it have become the masters of a great part of the world, which they are at the present day. There was, in spite of all that fierceness, much kindness and good nature among them; there were rules of conduct such as no man could find fault with—rules which still govern English society to some extent. And there was opportunity enough for social amusement, social enjoyment, and the winning of public esteem by a noble life.

Still, even in the "Havamal," one is occasionally startled by teachings which show the darker side of Northern life, a life of perpetual vendetta. As in old Japan, no man could live under the same heaven with the murderer of his brother or father; vengeance was a duty even in the case of a friend. On the subject of enemies the "Havamal" gives not a little curious advice:

A man should never step a foot beyond his weapons; for he can never tell where, on his path without, he may need his spear.

A man, before he goes into a house, should look to and espy all the doorways (*so that he can find his way out quickly again*), for he can never know where foes may be sitting in another man's house.

Does not this remind us of the Japanese proverb that everybody has three enemies outside of his own door? But the meaning of the "Havamal" teaching is much more sinister. And when the man goes into the house, he is still told to be extremely watchful—to keep his ears and eyes open so that he may not be taken by surprise:

The wary guest keeps watchful silence; he listens with his ears and peers about with his eyes; thus does every wise man look about him.

One would think that men must have had very strong nerves to take comfort under such circum-

stances, but the poet tells us that the man who can
enjoy nothing must be both a coward and a fool.
Although a man was to keep watch to protect his
life, that was not a reason why he should be afraid
of losing it. There were but three things of which
a man should be particularly afraid. The first
was drink—because drink often caused a man to
lose control of his temper; the second was another
man's wife—repeatedly the reader is warned
never to make love to another man's wife; and
the third was thieves—men who would pretend
friendship for the purpose of killing and stealing.
The man who could keep constant watch over
himself and his surroundings was, of course, likely
to have the longest life.

Now in all countries there is a great deal of ethical teaching, and always has been, on the subject
of speech. The "Havamal" is full of teaching on
this subject—the necessity of silence, the danger
and the folly of reckless talk. You all know the
Japanese proverb that "the mouth is the front gate
of all misfortune." The Norse poet puts the same
truth into a grimmer shape: "The tongue works
death to the head." Here are a number of sayings on this subject:

He that is never silent talks much folly; a glib tongue,
unless it be bridled, will often talk a man into trouble.

Do not speak three angry words with a worse man; for
often the better man falls by the worse man's sword.

Smile thou in the face of the man thou trustest not, and
speak against thy mind.

This is of course a teaching of cunning; but it is the teaching, however immoral, that rules in English society to-day. In the old Norse, however, there were many reasons for avoiding a quarrel whenever possible—reasons which must have existed also in feudal Japan. A man might not care about losing his own life; but he had to be careful not to stir up a feud that might go on for a hundred years. Although there was a great deal of killing, killing always remained a serious matter, because for every killing there had to be a vengeance. It is true that the law exonerated the man who killed another, if he paid a certain blood-price; murder was not legally considered an unpardonable crime. But the family of the dead man would very seldom be satisfied with a payment; they would want blood for blood. Accordingly men had to be very cautious about quarreling, however brave they might personally be.

But all this caution about silence and about watchfulness did not mean that a man should be unable to speak to the purpose when speech was required. "A wise man," says the "Havamal," "should be able both to ask and to answer." There is a proverb which you know, to the effect that you can not shut the door upon another man's mouth. So says the Norse poet: "The sons of men can keep silence about nothing that passes among men; therefore a man should be able to take his own part, prudently and strongly." Says

the "Havamal": "A fool thinks he knows everything if he sits snug in his little corner; but he is
at a loss for words if the people put to him a
question." Elsewhere it is said: "Arch dunce is
he who can speak nought, for that is the mark of
a fool." And the sum of all this teaching about
the tongue is that men should never speak without
good reason, and then should speak to the point
strongly and wisely.

On the subject of fools there is a great deal in
the "Havamal"; but you must understand always
by the word fool, in the Northern sense, a man of
weak character who knows not what to do in time
of difficulty. That was a fool among those men,
and a dangerous fool; for in such a state of society
mistakes in act or in speech might reach to terrible
consequences. See these little observations about
fools:

Open-handed, bold-hearted men live most happily, they
never feel care; but a fool troubles himself about everything. The niggard pines for gifts.

A fool is awake all night, worrying about everything;
when the morning comes he is worn out, and all his troubles are just the same as before.

A fool thinks that all who smile upon him are his
friends, not knowing, when he is with wise men, who
there may be plotting against him.

If a fool gets a drink, all his mind is immediately displayed.

But it was not considered right for a man not

to drink, although drink was a dangerous thing. On the contrary, not to drink would have been thought a mark of cowardice and of incapacity for self-control. A man was expected even to get drunk if necessary, and to keep his tongue and his temper no matter how much he drank. The strong character would only become more cautious and more silent under the influence of drink; the weak man would immediately show his weakness. I am told the curious fact that in the English army at the present day officers are expected to act very much after the teaching of the old Norse poet; a man is expected to be able on occasion to drink a considerable amount of wine or spirits without showing the effects of it, either in his conduct or in his speech. "Drink thy share of mead; speak fair or not at all"—that was the old text, and a very sensible one in its way.

Laughter was also condemned, if indulged in without very good cause. "The miserable man whose mind is warped laughs at everything, not knowing what he ought to know, that he himself has no lack of faults." I need scarcely tell you that the English are still a very serious people, not disposed to laugh nearly so much as are the men of the more sympathetic Latin races. You will remember perhaps Lord Chesterfield's saying that since he became a man no man had ever seen him laugh. I remember about twenty years ago that there was published by some Englishman a very learned and very interesting little book, called "The Philosophy of Laughter," in which it was gravely asserted that all laughter was foolish. I must acknowledge, however, that no book ever made me laugh more than the volume in question.

The great virtue of the men of the North, according to the "Havamal," was indeed the virtue which has given to the English race its present great position among nations,—the simplest of all virtues, common sense. But common sense means much more than the words might imply to the Japanese students, or to any one unfamiliar with English idioms. Common sense, or mother-wit, means natural intelligence, as opposed to, and independent of, cultivated or educated intelligence. It means inherited knowledge; and inherited knowledge may take even the form of genius. It means foresight. It means intuitive knowledge of other people's character. It means cunning as well as broad comprehension. And the modern Englishman, in all times and in all countries, trusts especially to this faculty, which is very largely developed in the race to which he belongs. No Englishman believes in working from book learning. He suspects all theories, philosophical or other. He suspects everything new, and dislikes it, unless he can be compelled by the force of circumstances to see that this new thing has advantages over the old. Race-experience is what he invariably depends upon, whenever he can, whether in India,

in Egypt, or in Australia. His statesmen do not
consult historical precedents in order to decide
what to do: they first learn the facts as they are;
then they depend upon their own common sense,
not at all upon their university learning or upon
philosophical theories. And in the case of the
English nation, it must be acknowledged that this
instinctive method has been eminently successful.
When the "Havamal" speaks of wisdom it means
mother-wit, and nothing else; indeed, there was no
reading or writing to speak of in those times:

No man can carry better baggage on his journey than
wisdom.

There is no better friend than great common sense.

But the wise man should not show himself to
be wise without occasion. He should remember
that the majority of men are not wise, and he
should be careful not to show his superiority over
them unnecessarily. Neither should be despise
men who do not happen to be as wise as himself:

No man is so good but there is a flaw in him, nor so
bad as to be good for nothing.

Middling wise should every man be; never overwise.
Those who know many things rarely lead the happiest life.

Middling wise should every man be; never overwise.
No man should know his fate beforehand; so shall he live
freest from care.

Middling wise should every man be, never too wise. A
wise man's heart is seldom glad, if its owner be a true sage.

This is the ancient wisdom also of Solomon:
"He that increases wisdom increases sorrow."
But how very true as worldly wisdom these little
Northern sentences are. That a man who knows
a little of many things, and no one thing perfectly,
is the happiest man—this certainly is even more
true to-day than it was a thousand years ago.
Spencer has well observed that the man who can
influence his generation, is never the man greatly
in advance of his time, but only the man who is
very slightly better than his fellows. The man
who is very superior is likely to be ignored or
disliked. Mediocrity can not help disliking superiority; and as the old Northern sage declared,
"the average of men is but moiety." Moiety does
not mean necessarily mediocrity, but also that
which is below mediocrity. What we call in England to-day, as Matthew Arnold called it, the Phi-
listine element, continues to prove in our own
time, to almost every superior man, the danger of
being too wise.

Interesting in another way, and altogether more
agreeable, are the old sayings about friendship:
"Know this, if thou hast a trusty friend, go
and see him often; because a road which is
seldom trod gets choked with brambles and
high grass."

Be not thou the first to break off from thy friend.
Sorrow will eat thy heart if thou lackest the friend to
open thy heart to.

Anything is better than to be false; he is no friend who only speaks to please.

Which means, of course, that a true friend is not afraid to find fault with his friend's course; indeed, that is his solemn duty. But these teachings about friendship are accompanied with many cautions; for one must be very careful in the making of friends. The ancient Greeks had a terrible proverb: "Treat your friend as if he should become some day your enemy; and treat your enemy as if he might some day become your friend." This proverb seems to me to indicate a certain amount of doubt in human nature. We do not find this doubt in the Norse teaching, but on the contrary, some very excellent advice. The first thing to remember is that friendship is sacred: "He that opens his heart to another mixes blood with him." Therefore one should be very careful either about forming or about breaking a friendship.

A man should be a friend to his friend's friend. But no man should be a friend of his friend's foe, nor of his foe's friend.

A man should be a friend with his friend, and pay back gift with gift; give back laughter for laughter (to his enemies), and lesing for lies.

Give and give back makes the longest friend. Give not overmuch at one time. Gift always looks for return.

The poet also tells us how trifling gifts are quite

sufficient to make friends and to keep them, if
wisely given. A costly gift may seem like a bribe;
a little gift is only the sign of kindly feeling. And
as a mere matter of justice, a costly gift may be
unkind, for it puts the friend under an obligation
which he may not be rich enough to repay. Repeatedly we are told also that too much should
not be expected of friendship. The value of a
friend is his affection, his sympathy; but favours
that cost must always be returned.

I never met a man so open-hearted and free with his
food, but that boon was boon to him—nor so generous as
not to look for return if he had a chance.

Emerson says almost precisely the same thing
in his essay on friendship—showing how little
human wisdom has changed in all the centuries.
Here is another good bit of advice concerning
visits:

It is far away to an ill friend, even though he live on
one's road; but to a good friend there is a short cut, even
though he live far out.

Go on, be not a guest ever in the same house. The
welcome becomes wearisome if he sits too long at another's
table.

This means that we must not impose on our
friends; but there is a further caution on the subject of eating at a friend's house. You must not
go to your friend's house hungry, when you can
help it.

A man should take his meal betimes, before he goes to his neighbour—or he will sit and seem hungered like one starving, and have no power to talk.

That is the main point to remember in dining at another's house, that you are not there only for your own pleasure, but for that of other people. You are expected to talk; and you can not talk if you are very hungry. At this very day a gentleman makes it the rule to do the same thing. Accordingly we see that these rough men of the North must have had a good deal of social refinement—refinement not of dress or of speech, but of feeling. Still, says the poet, one's own home is the best, though it be but a cottage. "A man is a man in his own house."

Now we come to some sentences teaching caution, which are noteworthy in a certain way:

Tell one man thy secret, but not two. What three men know, all the world knows.

Never let a bad man know thy mishaps; for from a bad man thou shalt never get reward for thy sincerity.

I shall presently give you some modern examples in regard to the advice concerning bad men. Another thing to be cautious about is praise. If you have to be careful about blame, you must be very cautious also about praise.

Praise the day at even-tide; a woman at her burying; a sword when it has been tried; a maid when she is married; ice when you have crossed over it; ale when it is drunk.

If there is anything noteworthy in English character to-day it is the exemplification of this very kind of teaching. This is essentially Northern. The last people from whom praise can be expected, even for what is worthy of all praise, are the English. A new friendship, a new ideal, a reform, a noble action, a wonderful poet, an exquisite painting—any of these things will be admired and praised by every other people in Europe long before you can get Englishmen to praise. The Englishman all this time is studying, considering, trying to find fault. Why should he try to find fault? So that he will not make any mistakes at a later day. He has inherited the terrible caution of his ancestors in regard to mistakes. It must be granted that his caution has saved him from a number of very serious mistakes that other nations have made. It must also be acknowledged that he exercises a fair amount of moderation in the opposite direction—this modern Englishman; he has learned caution of another kind, which his ancestors taught him. "Power," says the "Havamal," "should be used with moderation; for whoever finds himself among valiant men will discover that no man is peerless." And this is a very important thing for the strong man to know—that however strong, he can not be the strongest; his match will be found when occasion demands it.

Not only Scandinavian but English rulers have often discovered this fact to their cost. Another matter to be very anxious about is public opinion.

Chattels die; kinsmen pass away; one dies oneself; but I know something that never dies—the name of the man, for good or bad.

Do not think that this means anything religious. It means only that the reputation of a man goes to influence the good or ill fortune of his descendants. It is something to be proud of, to be the son of a good man; it helps to success in life. On the other hand, to have had a father of ill reputation is a very serious obstacle to success of any kind in countries where the influence of heredity is strongly recognized.

I have nearly exhausted the examples of this Northern wisdom which I selected for you; but there are two subjects which remain to be considered. One is the law of conduct in regard to misfortune; and the other is the rule of conduct in regard to women. A man was expected to keep up a brave heart under any circumstances. These old Northmen seldom committed suicide; and I must tell you that all the talk about Christianity having checked the practice of suicide to some extent, can not be fairly accepted as truth. In modern England to-day the suicides average nearly three thousand a year; but making allowance for extraordinary circumstances, it is certainly true that the Northern races consider suicide in an entirely different way from what the Latin races do. There was very little suicide among the men of the North, because every man considered it his duty to get killed, not to kill himself; and to kill himself would have seemed cowardly, as implying fear of being killed by others. In modern ethical training, quite apart from religious considerations, a man is taught that suicide is only excusable in case of shame, or under such exceptional circumstances as have occurred in the history of the Indian mutiny. At all events, we have the feeling still strongly manifested in England that suicide is not quite manly; and this is certainly due much more to ancestral habits of thinking, which date back to pagan days, than to Christian doctrine. As I have said, the pagan English would not commit suicide to escape mere pain. But the Northern people knew how to die to escape shame. There is an awful story in Roman history about the wives and daughters of the conquered German tribes, thousands in number, asking to be promised that their virtue should be respected, and all killing themselves when the Roman general refused the request. No Southern people of Europe in that time would have shown such heroism upon such a matter. Leaving honour aside, however, the old book tells us that a man should never despair.

Fire, the sight of the sun, good health, and a blameless life,—these are the goodliest things in this world.

Yet a man is not utterly wretched, though he have bad health, or be maimed.

The halt may ride a horse; the handless may drive a herd; the deaf can fight and do well; better be blind than buried. A corpse is good for naught.

On the subject of women there is not very much in the book beyond the usual caution in regard to wicked women; but there is this little observation:

Never blame a woman for what is all man's weakness. Hues charming and fair may move the wise and not the dullard. Mighty love turns the son of men from wise to fool.

This is shrewd, and it contains a very remarkable bit of esthetic truth, that it requires a wise man to see certain kinds of beauty, which a stupid man could never be made to understand. And, leaving aside the subject of love, what very good advice it is never to laugh at a person for what can be considered a common failure. In the same way an intelligent man should learn to be patient with the unintelligent, as the same poem elsewhere insists.

Now what is the general result of this little study, the general impression that it leaves upon the mind? Certainly we feel that the life reflected in these sentences was a life in which caution was above all things necessary—caution in thought and speech and act, never ceasing, by night or day, during the whole of a man's life. Caution implies moderation. Moderation inevitably develops a certain habit of justice—a justice that might not extend outside of the race, but a justice that would be exercised between man and man of the same blood. Very much of English character and of English history is explained by the life that the "Havamal" portrays. Very much that is good; also very much that is bad—not bad in one sense, so far as the future of the race is concerned, but in a social way certainly not good. The judgment of the Englishman by all other European peoples is that he is the most suspicious, the most reserved, the most unreceptive, the most unfriendly, the coldest hearted, and the most domineering of all Western peoples. Ask a Frenchman, an Italian, a German, a Spaniard, even an American, what he thinks about Englishmen; and every one of them will tell you the very same thing. This is precisely what the character of men would become who had lived for thousands of years in the conditions of Northern society. But you would find upon the other hand that nearly all nations would speak highly of certain other English qualities—energy, courage, honour, justice (between themselves). They would say that although no man is so difficult to make friends with, the friendship of an

Englishman once gained is more strong and true than any other. And as the battle of life still continues, and must continue for thousands of years to come, it must be acknowledged that the English character is especially well fitted for the struggle. Its reserves, its cautions, its doubts, its suspicions, its brutality—these have been for it in the past, and are still in the present, the best social armour and panoply of war. It is not a lovable nor an amiable character; it is not even kindly. The Englishman of the best type is much more inclined to be just than he is to be kind, for kindness is an emotional impulse, and the Englishman is on his guard against every kind of emotional impulse. But with all this, the character is a grand one, and its success has been the best proof of its value.

Now you will have observed in the reading of this ancient code of social morals that, while none of the teaching is religious, some of it is absolutely immoral from any religious standpoint. No great religion permits us to speak what is not true, and to smile in the face of an enemy while pretending to be his friend. No religion teaches that we should "pay back lesing for lies." Neither does a religion tell us that we should expect a return for every kindness done; that we should regard friendship as being actuated by selfish motives; that we should never praise when praise seems to be deserved. In fact, when Sir Walter Scott long ago made a partial translation of the "Havamal," he thought himself obliged to leave out a number of sentences which seemed to him highly immoral, and to apologize for others. He thought that they would shock English readers too much.

We are not quite so squeamish to-day; and a thinker of our own time would scarcely deny that English society is very largely governed at this moment by the same kind of rules that Sir Walter Scott thought to be so bad. But here we need not condemn English society in particular. All European society has been for hundreds of years conducting itself upon very much the same principles; for the reason that human social experience has been the same in all Western countries. I should say that the only difference between English society and other societies is that the hardness of character is very much greater. Let us go back even to the most Christian times of Western societies in the most Christian country of Europe, and observe whether the social code was then and there so very different from the social code of the old "Havamal." Mr. Spencer observes in his "Ethics" that, so far as the conduct of life is concerned, religion is almost nothing and practice is everything. We find this wonderfully exemplified in a most remarkable book of social precepts written in the seventeenth century, in Spain, under the title of the "Oraculo Manual." It was composed by a Spanish priest, named Baltasar Gracian, who

was born in the year 1601 and died in 1658; and
it has been translated into nearly all languages.
The best English translation, published by Mac-
millan, is called "The Art of Worldly Wisdom."
It is even more admired to-day than in the seventeenth century; and what it teaches as to social
conduct holds as good to-day of modern society as
it did of society two hundred years ago. It is one
of the most unpleasant and yet interesting books
ever published—unpleasant because of the malicious cunning which it often displays—interesting
because of the frightful perspicacity of the author.
The man who wrote that book understood the
hearts of men, especially the bad side. He was a
gentleman of high rank before he became a priest,
and his instinctive shrewdness must have been
hereditary. Religion, this man would have said,
teaches the best possible morals; but the world is
not governed by religion altogether, and to mix
with it, we must act according to its dictates.

These dictates remind us in many ways of the
cautions and the cunning of the "Havamal." The
first thing enjoined upon a man both by the Norse
writer and by the Spanish author is the art of
silence. Probably this has been the result of social experience in all countries. "Cautious silence
is the holy of holies of worldly wisdom," says
Gracian. And he gives many elaborate reasons
for this statement, not the least of which is the
following: "If you do not declare yourself im-

mediately, you arouse expectation, especially when
the importance of your position makes you the object of general attention. Mix a little mystery
with everything, and the very mystery arouses ven-
eration." A little further on he gives us exactly
the same advice as did the "Havamal" writer, in
regard to being frank with enemies. "Do not,"
he says, "show your wounded finger, for everything will knock up against it; nor complain about
it, for malice always aims where weakness can be
injured. . . . Never disclose the source of mor-
tification or of joy, if you wish the one to cease,
the other to endure." About secrets the Spaniard
is quite as cautious as the Norseman. He says,
"Especially dangerous are secrets entrusted to
friends. He that communicates his secret to another makes himself that other man's slave." But
after a great many such cautions in regard to silence and secrecy, he tells us also that we must
learn how to fight with the world. You remember
the advice of the "Havamal" on this subject, how
it condemns as a fool the man who can not answer
a reproach. The Spaniard is, however, much
more malicious in his suggestions. He tells us
that we must "learn to know every man's thumbscrew." I suppose you know that a thumbscrew
was an instrument of torture used in old times to
force confessions from criminals. This advice
means nothing less than that we should learn how

to be able to hurt other men's feelings, or to flatter
other men's weaknesses. "First guess every
man's ruling passion, appeal to it by a word, set
it in motion by temptation, and you will infallibly
give checkmate to his freedom of will." The term
"give checkmate" is taken from the game of
chess, and must here be understood as meaning to
overcome, to conquer. A kindred piece of advice
is "keep a store of sarcasms, and know how to
use them." Indeed he tells us that this is the
point of greatest tact in human intercourse.
"Struck by the slightest word of this kind, many
fall away from the closest intimacy with superiors
or inferiors, which intimacy could not be in the
slightest shaken by a whole conspiracy of popular
insinuation or private malevolence." In other
words, you can more quickly destroy a man's
friendship by one word of sarcasm than by any
amount of intrigue. Does not this read very much
like sheer wickedness? Certainly it does; but the
author would have told you that you must fight the
wicked with their own weapons. In the "Havamal" you will not find anything quite so openly
wicked as that; but we must suppose that the
Norsemen knew the secret, though they might not
have put it into words. As for the social teaching, you will find it very subtly expressed even in
the modern English novels of George Meredith,
who, by the way, has written a poem in praise of

sarcasm and ridicule. But let us now see what
the Spanish author has to tell us about friendship
and unselfishness.

The shrewd man knows that others when they
seek him do not seek "him," but "their advantage
in him and by him." That is to say, a shrewd man
does not believe in disinterested friendship. This
is much worse than anything in the "Havamal."
And it is diabolically elaborated. What are we
to say about such teaching as the following: "A
wise man would rather see men needing him than
thanking him. To keep them on the threshold
of hope is diplomatic; to trust to their gratitude
is boorish; hope has a good memory, gratitude a
bad one"? There is much more of this kind; but
after the assurance that only a boorish person
(that is to say, an ignorant and vulgar man) can
believe in gratitude, the author's opinion of human
nature needs no further elucidation. The old
Norseman would have been shocked at such a
statement. But he might have approved the following: "When you hear anything favourable,
keep a tight rein upon your credulity; if unfavour-
able, give it the spur." That is to say, when you
hear anything good about another man, do not be
ready to believe it; but if you hear anything bad
about him, believe as much of it as you can.

I notice also many other points of resemblance
between the Northern and the Spanish teaching in
regard to caution. The "Havamal" says that you

must not pick a quarrel with a worse man than
yourself; "because the better man often falls by
the worse man's sword." The Spanish priest
gives a still shrewder reason for the same policy.
"Never contend," he says, "with a man who has
nothing to lose; for thereby you enter into an un-
equal conflict. The other enters without anxiety;
having lost everything, including shame, he has no
further loss to fear." I think that this is an immoral teaching, though a very prudent one; but I
need scarcely to tell you that it is still a principle
in modern society not to contend with a man who
has no reputation to lose. I think it is immoral,
because it is purely selfish, and because a good man
ought not to be afraid to denounce a wrong because of making enemies. Another point, however, on which the "Havamal" and the priest
agree, is more commendable and interesting. "We
do not think much of a man who never contradicts
us; that is no sign he loves us, but rather a sign
that he loves himself. Original and out-of-the-
way views are signs of superior ability."

I should not like you to suppose, however, that
the whole of the book from which I have been
quoting is of the same character as the quotations.
There is excellent advice in it; and much kindly
teaching on the subject of generous acts. It is a
book both good and bad, and never stupid. The
same man who tells you that friendship is seldom
unselfish, also declares that life would be a desert

without friends, and that there is no magic like a
good turn—that is, a kind act. He teaches the importance of getting good will by honest means, although he advises us also to learn how to injure.
I am sure that nobody could read the book without benefit. And I may close these quotations
from it with the following paragraph, which is
the very best bit of counsel that could be given
to a literary student:

> Be slow and sure. Quickly done can be quickly undone.
> To last an eternity requires an eternity of preparation.
> Only excellence counts. Profound intelligence is the only
> foundation for immortality. Worth much costs much.
> The precious metals are the heaviest.

But so far as the question of human conduct is
concerned, the book of Gracian is no more of a
religious book than is the "Havamal" of the
heathen North. You would find, were such a book
published to-day and brought up to the present
time by any shrewd writer, that Western morality
has not improved in the least since the time before
Christianity was established, so far as the rules of
society go. Society is not, and can not be, religious, because it is a state of continual warfare.
Every person in it has to fight, and the battle is
not less cruel now because it is not fought with
swords. Indeed, I should think that the time when
every man carried his sword in society was a time
when men were quite as kindly and much more

honest than they are now. The object of this little lecture was to show you that the principles of the ancient Norse are really the principles ruling English society to-day; but I think you will be able to take from it a still larger meaning. It is that not only one form of society, but all forms of society, represent the warfare of man and man. That is why thinkers, poets, philosophers, in all ages, have tried to find solitude, to keep out of the contest, to devote themselves only to study of the beautiful and the true. But the prizes of life are not to be obtained in solitude, although the prizes of thought can only there be won. After all, whatever we may think about the cruelty and treachery of the social world, it does great things in the end. It quickens judgment, deepens intelligence, enforces the acquisition of self-control, creates forms of mental and moral strength that can not fail to be sometimes of vast importance to mankind. But if you should ask me whether it increases human happiness, I should certainly say "no." The "Havamal" said the same thing,—the truly wise man can not be happy.

CHAPTER VIII

BEYOND MAN

It seems to me a lecturer's duty to speak to you about any remarkable thought at this moment engaging the attention of Western philosophers and men of science,—partly because any such new ideas are certain, sooner or later, to be reflected in literature, and partly because without a knowledge of them you might form incorrect ideas in relation to utterances of any important philosophic character. I am not going to discourse about Nietzsche, though the title of this lecture is taken from one of his books; the ideas about which I am going to tell you, you will not find in his books. It is most extraordinary, to my thinking, that these ideas never occurred to him, for he was an eminent man of science before writing his probably insane books. I have not the slightest sympathy with most of his ideas; they seem to me misinterpretations of evolutional teachings; and if not misinterpretations, they are simply undeveloped and ill-balanced thinking. But the title of one of his books, and the idea which he tries always unsuccessfully to explain,—that of a state above mankind, a moral condition "beyond man," as he calls it,—that is worth talking about. It is not nonsense at all, but fact, and I think that I can give you a correct idea of the realities in the case. Leaving Nietzsche entirely alone, then, let us ask if it is possible to suppose a condition of human existence above morality,—that is to say, more moral than the most moral ideal which a human brain can conceive? We may answer, it is quite possible, and it is not only possible, but it has actually been predicted by many great thinkers, including Herbert Spencer.

We have been brought up to think that there can be nothing better than virtue, than duty, than strictly following the precepts of a good religion. However, our ideas of goodness and of virtue necessarily imply the existence of the opposite qualities. To do a good thing because it is our duty to do it, implies a certain amount of resolve, a struggle against difficulty. The virtue of honesty is a term implying the difficulty of being perfectly honest. When we think of any virtuous or great deed, we can not help thinking of the pain and obstacles that have to be met with in performing that deed. All our active morality is a struggle against immorality. And I think that, as every religion teaches, it must be granted that no human being has a perfectly moral nature.

Could a world exist in which the nature of all the inhabitants would be so moral that the mere idea of what is immoral could not exist? Let me explain my question more in detail. Imagine a society in which the idea of dishonesty would not exist, because no person could be dishonest, a society in which the idea of unchastity could not exist, because no person could possibly be unchaste, a world in which no one could have any idea of envy, ambition or anger, because such passions could not exist, a world in which there would be no idea of duty, filial or parental, because not to be filial, not to be loving, not to do everything which we human beings now call duty, would be impossible. In such a world ideas of duty would be quite useless; for every action of existence would represent the constant and faultless performance of what we term duty. Moreover, there would be no difficulty, no pain in such performance; it would be the constant and unfailing pleasure of life. With us, unfortunately, what is wrong often gives pleasure; and what is good to do, commonly causes pain. But in the world which I am asking you to imagine there could not be any wrong, nor any pleasure in wrong-doing; all the pleasure would be in right-doing. To give a very simple illustration—one of the commonest and most pardonable faults of young people is eating, drinking, or sleeping too much. But in our imaginary world to eat or to drink or to sleep in even the least degree more than is necessary could not be done; the constitution of the race would not permit it. One more illustration. Our children have to be educated carefully in regard to what is right or wrong; in the world of which I am speaking, no time would be wasted in any such education, for every child would be born with full knowledge of what is right and wrong. Or to state the case in psychological language—I mean the language of scientific, not of metaphysical, psychology—we should have a world in which morality would have been transmuted into inherited instinct. Now again let me put the question: can we imagine such a world? Perhaps you will answer, Yes, in heaven—nowhere else. But I answer you that such a world actually exists, and that it can be studied in almost any part of the East or of Europe by a person of scientific training. The world of insects actually furnishes examples of such a moral transformation. It is for this reason that such writers as Sir John Lubbock and Herbert Spencer have not hesitated to say that certain kinds of social insects have immensely surpassed men, both in social and in ethical progress.

But that is not all that it is necessary to say here. You might think that I am only repeating a kind of parable. The important thing is the opinion of scientific men that humanity will at last, in the course of millions of years, reach the ethical conditions of the ants. It is only five or six years ago that some of these conditions were established by scientific evidence, and I want to

speak of them.   They have a direct bearing upon
important ethical questions; and they have startled the whole moral world, and set men thinking
in entirely new directions.

In order to explain how the study of social insects has set moralists of recent years thinking in
a new direction, it will be necessary to generalize
a great deal in the course of so short a lecture.   It
is especially the social conditions of the ants which
has inspired these new ideas; but you must not
think that any one species of ants furnishes us with
all the facts.   The facts have been arrived at only
through the study of hundreds of different kinds
of ants by hundreds of scientific men; and it is only
by the consensus of their evidence that we get the
ethical picture which I shall try to outline for you.
Altogether there are probably about five thousand
different species of ants, and these different species
represent many different stages of social evolution, from the most primitive and savage up to the
most highly civilized and moral.   The details of
the following picture are furnished by a number
of the highest species only; that must not be forgotten.   Also, I must remind you that the morality of the ant, by the necessity of circumstance,
does not extend beyond the limits of its own species.   Impeccably ethical within the community,
ants carry on war outside their own borders; were
it not for this, we might call them morally perfect
creatures.

Although the mind of an ant can not be at all

like the mind of the human being, it is so intelligent that we are justified in trying to describe its existence by a kind of allegorical comparison with human life. Imagine, then, a world full of women, working night and day,—building, tunnelling, bridging,—also engaged in agriculture, in horticulture, and in taking care of many kinds of domestic animals. (I may remark that ants have domesticated no fewer than five hundred and eighty-four different kinds of creatures.) This world of women is scrupulously clean; busy as they are, all of them carry combs and brushes about them, and arrange themselves several times a day. In addition to this constant work, these women have to take care of myriads of children,—children so delicate that the slightest change in the weather may kill them. So the children have to be carried constantly from one place to another in order to keep them warm.

Though this multitude of workers are always gathering food, no one of them would eat or drink a single atom more than is necessary; and none of them would sleep for one second longer than is necessary. Now comes a surprising fact, about which a great deal must be said later on. These women have no sex. They are women, for they sometimes actually give birth, as virgins, to children; but they are incapable of wedlock. They are more than vestals. Sex is practically suppressed.

This world of workers is protected by an army

of soldiers. The soldiers are very large, very strong, and shaped so differently from the working females that they do not seem at first to belong to the same race. They help in the work, though they are not able to help in some delicate kinds of work—they are too clumsy and strong. Now comes the second astonishing fact: these soldiers are all women—amazons, we might call them; but they are sexless women. In these also sex has been suppressed.

You ask, where do the children come from? Most of the children are born of special mothers —females chosen for the purpose of bearing offspring, and not allowed to do anything else. They are treated almost like empresses, being constantly fed and attended and served, and being lodged in the best way possible. Only these can eat and drink at all times—they must do so for the sake of their offspring. They are not suffered to go out, unless strongly attended, and they are not allowed to run any risk of danger or of injury. The life of the whole race circles about them and about their children, but they are very few.

Last of all are the males, the men. One naturally asks why females should have been specialized into soldiers instead of men. It appears that the females have more reserve force, and all the force that might have been utilized in the giving of life has been diverted to the making of aggressive powers. The real males are very small and weak. They appear to be treated with indifference and contempt. They are suffered to become the bridegrooms of one night, after which they die very quickly. By contrast, the lives of the rest are very long. Ants live for at least three or four years, but the males live only long enough to perform their solitary function.

In the foregoing little fantasy, the one thing that should have most impressed you is the fact of the suppression of sex. But now comes the last and most astonishing fact of all: this suppression of sex is not natural, but artificial—I mean that it is voluntary. It has been discovered that ants are able, by a systematic method of nourishment, to suppress or develop sex as they please. The race has decided that sex shall not be allowed to exist except in just so far as it is absolutely necessary to the existence of the race. Individuals with sex are tolerated only as necessary evils. Here is an instance of the most powerful of all passions voluntarily suppressed for the benefit of the community at large. It vanishes whenever unnecessary; when necessary after a war or a calamity of some kind, it is called into existence again. Certainly it is not wonderful that such a fact should have set moralists thinking. Of course if a human community could discover some secret way of effecting the same object, and could have the courage to do it, or rather the unselfishness to do it, the result would simply be that sexual immorality of any kind would become practically impossible. The very idea of such immorality would cease to exist.

But that is only one fact of self-suppression, and the ant-world furnishes hundreds. To state the whole thing in the simplest possible way, let me say the race has entirely got rid of everything that we call a selfish impulse. Even hunger and thirst allow of no selfish gratification. The entire life of the community is devoted to the common good and to mutual help and to the care of the young. Spencer says it is impossible to imagine that an ant has a sense of duty like our own,—a religion, if you like. But it does not need a sense of duty, it does not need religion. Its life is religion in the practical sense. Probably millions of years ago the ant had feelings much more like our own than it has now. At that time, to perform altruistic actions may have been painful to the ant; to perform them now has become the one pleasure of its existence. In order to bring up children and serve the state more efficiently these insects have sacrificed their sex and every appetite that we call by the name of animal passion. Moreover they have a perfect community, a society in which nobody could think of property, except as a state affair, a public thing, or as the Romans would say, a *res publica*. In a human community so organized, there could not be ambition, any jealousy, any selfish conduct of any sort—indeed, no selfishness at all. The individual is said to be practically sacrificed for the sake of the race; but such a supposition means the highest moral altruism. Therefore thinkers have to ask, "Will man ever rise to something like the condition of ants?"

Herbert Spencer says that such is the evident tendency. He does not say, nor is it at all probable, that there will be in future humanity such physiological specialization as would correspond to the suppression of sex among ants, or to the bringing of women to the dominant place in the human world, and the masculine sex to an inferior position. That is not likely ever to happen, for reasons which it would take very much too long to speak of now. But there is evidence that the most selfish of all human passions will eventually be brought under control—under such control that the present cause of wellnigh all human suffering, the pressure of population, will be practically removed. And there is psychological evidence that the human mind will undergo such changes that wrong-doing, in the sense of unkindly action, will become almost impossible, and that the highest pleasure will be found not in selfishness but in unselfishness. Of course there are thousands of things to think about, suggested by this discovery of the life of ants. I am only telling the more important ones. What I have told you ought at least to suggest that the idea of a moral condition much higher than all our moral conditions of to-day is quite possible,—that it is not an idea to be laughed at. But it was not Nietzsche who ever conceived this possibility. His "Beyond Man," and the real and much to be hoped for "beyond man," are absolutely antagonistic conceptions. When the ancient Hebrew writer said, thousands of years ago, "Go to the ant, thou sluggard, consider her ways," he could not have imagined how good his advice would prove in the light of twentieth century science.

CHAPTER IX

THE NEW ETHICS

BEFORE leaving the subject of these latter-day intellectual changes, a word must be said concerning the ethical questions involved. Of course when a religious faith has been shaken to its foundation, it is natural to suppose that morals must have been simultaneously affected. The relation of morals to literature is very intimate; and we must expect that any change of ideas in the direction of ethics would show themselves in literature. The drama, poetry, romance, the novel, all these are reflections of moral emotion in especial, of the eternal struggle between good and evil, as well as of the temporary sentiments concerning right and wrong. And every period of transition is necessarily accompanied by certain tendencies to disintegration. Contemporary literature in the West has shown some signs of ethical change. These caused many thinkers to predict a coming period of demoralization in literature. But the alarm was really quite needless. These vagaries of literature, such as books questioning the morality of the marriage relation, for example, were only repetitions of older vagaries, and represented

145

nothing more than the temporary agitation
of thought upon all questions. The fact
seems to be that in spite of everything, moral feeling was never higher at any time in Western social
history than it is at present. The changes of
thought have indeed been very great, but the
moral experience of mankind remains exactly as
valuable as it was before, and new perceptions of
that value have been given to us by the new
philosophy.

It has been wisely observed by the greatest of
modern thinkers that mankind has progressed
more rapidly in every other respect than in morality. Moral progress has not been rapid simply
because the moral ideal has always been kept a
little in advance of the humanly possible. Thousands of years ago the principles of morality were
exactly the same as those which rule our lives
to-day. We can not improve upon them; we
can not even improve upon the language which
expressed them. The most learned of our poets
could not make a more beautiful prayer than the
prayer which Egyptian mothers taught to their
little children in ages when all Europe was still a
land of savages. The best of the moral philosophy of the nineteenth century is very little of improvement upon the moral philosophy of ancient
India or China. If there is any improvement at
all, it is simply in the direction of knowledge of
causes and effects. And that is why in all coun-

tries the common sense of mankind universaliy condemns any attempt to interfere with moral ideas. These represent the social experience of man for thousands and thousands of years; and it is not likely that the wisdom of any one individual can ever better them. If bettered at all it can not be through theory. The amelioration must be effected by future experience of a universal kind. We may improve every branch of science, every branch of art, everything else relating to the work of human heads and hands; but we can not improve morals by invention or by hypothesis. Morals are not made, but grow.

Yet, as I have said, there is what may be called a new system of ethics. But this new system of ethics means nothing more than a new way of understanding the old system of ethics. By the application of evolutional science to the study of morals, we have been enabled to trace back the whole history of moral ideas to the time of their earliest inception,—to understand the reasons of them, and to explain them without the help of any supernatural theory. And the result, so far from diminishing our respect for the wisdom of our ancestors, has immensely increased that respect. There is no single moral teaching common to different civilizations and different religions of an advanced stage of development which we do not find to be eternally true. Let us try to study this view of the case by the help of a few examples.

In early times, of course, men obeyed moral instruction through religious motives. If asked why
they thought it was wrong to perform certain actions and right to perform others, they could have
answered only that such was ancestral custom and
that the gods will it so. Not until we could understand the laws governing the evolution of society could we understand the reason of many
ethical regulations. But now we can understand
very plainly that the will of the gods, as our ancestors might have termed it, represents divine
laws indeed, for the laws of ethical evolution are
certainly the unknown laws shaping all things—
suns, worlds, and human societies. All that op-
poses itself to the operation of those universal
laws is what we have been accustomed to call bad,
and everything which aids the operation of those
laws is what we have been accustomed to think of
as good. The common crimes condemned by all
religions, such as theft, murder, adultery, bearing
false witness, disloyalty, all these are practices
which directly interfere with the natural process
of evolution; and without understanding why,
men have from the earliest times of real civilization united all their power to suppress them. I
think that we need not dwell upon the simple
facts; they will at once suggest to you all that is
necessary to know. I shall select for illustration
only one less familiar topic, that of the ascetic
ideal.

A great many things which in times of lesser knowledge we imagined to be superstitious or useless, prove to-day on examination to have been of immense value to mankind. Probably no superstition ever existed which did not have some social value; and the most seemingly repulsive or cruel sometimes turn out to have been the most precious. To choose one of these for illustration, we must take one not confined to any particular civilization or religion, but common to all human societies at a certain period of their existence; and the ascetic ideal best fits our purpose. From very early times, even from a time long preceding any civilization, we find men acting under the idea that by depriving themselves of certain pleasures and by subjecting themselves to certain pains they could please the divine powers and thereby obtain strength. Probably there is no people in the world among whom this belief has not had at some one time or another a very great influence. At a later time, in the early civilizations, this idea would seem to have obtained much larger sway, and to have affected national life more and more extensively. In the age of the great religions the idea reaches its acme, an acme often represented by extravagances of the most painful kind and sacrifices which strike modern imagination as ferocious and terrible. In Europe asceticism reached its great extremes as you know during the Middle Ages, and especially took the direction of antagonism to the natural sex-relation. Looking back to-day to the centuries in which celibacy was considered the most moral condition, and marriage was counted as little better than weakness, when Europe was covered with thousands of monasteries, and when the best intellects of the age deemed it the highest duty to sacrifice everything pleasurable for the sake of an imaginary reward after death, we can not but recognize that we are contemplating a period of religious insanity. Even in the architecture of the time, the architecture that Ruskin devoted his splendid talent to praise, there is a grim and terrible something that suggests madness. Again, the cruelties of the age have an insane character, the burning alive of myriads of people who refused to believe or could not believe in the faith of their time; the tortures used to extort confessions from the innocent; the immolation of thousands charged with being wizards or witches; the extinction of little centres of civilization in the South of France and elsewhere by brutal crusades—contemplating all this, we seem to be contemplating not only madness but furious madness. I need not speak to you of the Crusades, which also belonged to this period. Compared with the Roman and Greek civilizations before it, what a horrible Europe it was! And yet the thinker must recognize that it had a strength of its own, a strength of a larger kind than that of the preceding civilizations. It may seem monstrous to assert that all this cruelty and superstition and contempt of learning were absolutely necessary for the progress of mankind; and yet we must so accept them in the light of modern knowledge. The checking of intellectual development for hundreds of years is certainly a fact that must shock us; but the true question is whether such a checking had not become necessary. Intellectual strength, unless supported by moral strength, leads a people into the ways of destruction. Compared with the men of the Middle Ages, the Greeks and Romans were incomparably superior intellectually; compared with them morally they were very weak. They had conquered the world and developed all the arts, these Greeks and Romans; they had achieved things such as mankind has never since been able to accomplish, and then, losing their moral ideal, losing their simplicity, losing their faith, they were utterly crushed by inferior races in whom the principles of self-denial had been intensely developed. And the old instinctive hatred of the Church for the arts and the letters and the sciences of the Greek and Roman civilizations was not quite so much of a folly as we might be apt to suppose. The priests recognized in a vague way that anything like a revival of the older civilizations would signify moral ruin. The Renaissance proves that the priests were not wrong. Had the movement occurred a few hundred years earlier, the result

would probably have been a universal corruption.
I do not mean to say that the Church at any time
was exactly conscious of what she was doing; she
acted blindly under the influence of an instinctive
fear.   But the result of all that she did has not
proved unfortunate.   What the Roman and Greek
civilizations had lost in moral power was given
back to the world by the frightful discipline of the
Middle Ages.   For a long series of generations
the ascetic idea was triumphant; and it became
feeble only in proportion as men became strong
enough to do without it.   Especially it remodelled
that of which it first seemed the enemy, the family relation.   It created a new basis for society,
founded upon a new sense of the importance to
society of family morals.   Because this idea, this
morality, came through superstitution, its value
is not thereby in the least diminished.   Superstitions often represent correct guesses at eternal
truth.   To-day we know that all social progress,
all national strength, all national vigour, intellectual as well as physical, depend essentially upon
the family, upon the morality of the household,
upon the relation of parents to children.   It was
this fact which the Greeks and Romans forgot,
and lost themselves by forgetting.   It was this
fact which the superstitious tyranny of the Middle
Ages had to teach the West over again, and after
such a fashion that it is not likely ever to become
forgotten.   So much for the mental history of the

question. Let us say a word about the physical aspects of it.

No doubt you have read that the result of macerating the body, of depriving oneself of all comfort, and even of nourishing food, is not an increase of intellectual vigour or moral power of any kind. And in one sense this is true. The individual who passes his life in self-mortification is not apt to improve under that régime. For this reason the founder of the greatest of Oriental religions condemned asceticism on the part of his followers, except within certain fixed limits. But the history of the changes produced by a universal idea is not a history of changes in the individual, but of changes brought about by the successive efforts of millions of individuals in the course of many generations. Not in one lifetime can we perceive the measure of ethical force obtained by self-control; but in the course of several hundreds of years we find that the result obtained is so large as to astonish us. This result, imperceptibly obtained, signifies a great increase of that nervous power upon which moral power depends; it means an augmentation in strength of every kind; and this augmentation again represents what we might call economy. Just as there is a science of political economy, there is a science of ethical economy; and it is in relation to such a science that we should rationally consider the influence of all religions teaching self-suppression. So studying, we find that self-suppression does not mean the destruction of any power, but only the economical storage of that power for the benefit of the race. As a result, the highly civilized man can endure incomparably more than the savage, whether of moral or physical strain. Being better able to control himself under all circumstances, he has a great advantage over the savage.

That which is going on in the new teaching of ethics is really the substitution of a rational for an emotional morality. But this does not mean that the value of the emotional element in morality is not recognized. Not only is it recognized, but it is even being enlarged—enlarged, however, in a rational way. For example, let us take the very emotional virtue of loyalty. Loyalty, in a rational form, could not exist among an uneducated people; it could only exist as a feeling, a sentiment. In the primitive state of society this sentiment takes the force and the depth of a religion. And the ruler, regarded as divine, really has in relation to his people the power of a god. Once that people becomes educated in the modern sense, their ideas regarding their ruler and their duties to their ruler necessarily undergo modification. But does this mean that the sentiment is weakened in the educated class? I should say that this depends very much upon the quality of the individual mind. In a mind of small capacity, incapable of receiving the higher forms of thought, it is very

likely that the sentiment may be weakened and
almost destroyed.   But in the mind of a real
thinker, a man of true culture, the sense of loyalty,
although changed, is at the same time immensely
expanded.   In order to give a strong example, I
should take the example not from a monarchical
country but from a republican one.   What does
the President of the United States of America, for
example, represent to the American of the highest
culture?   He appears to him in two entirely different capacities.   First he appears to him merely
as a man, an ordinary man, with faults and weaknesses like other ordinary men.   His private life is
apt to be discussed in the newspapers.   He is expected to shake hands with anybody and with
everybody whom he meets at Washington; and
when he ceases to hold office, he has no longer
any particular distinction from other Americans.
But as the President of the United States, he is
also much more than a man.   He represents one
hundred millions of people; he represents the
American Constitution; he represents the great
principles of human freedom laid down by that
Constitution; he represents also the idea of America, of everything American, of all the hopes, interests, and glories of the nation.   Officially he is
quite as sacred as a divinity could be.   Millions
would give their lives for him at an instant's notice; and thousands capable of making vulgar
jokes about the man would hotly resent the least

word spoken about the President as the representative of America. The very same thing exists in other Western countries, notwithstanding the fact that the lives of rulers are sometimes attempted. England is a striking example. The Queen has really scarcely any power; her rule is little more than nominal. Every Englishman knows that England is a monarchy only in name. But the Queen represents to every Englishman more than a woman and more than a queen: she represents England, English race feeling, English love of country, English power, English dignity; she is a symbol, and as a symbol sacred. The soldier jokingly calls her "the Widow"; he makes songs about her; all this is well and good. But a soldier who cursed her a few years ago was promptly sent to prison for twenty years. To sing a merry song about the sovereign as a woman is a right which English freedom claims; but to speak disrespectfully of the Queen, as England, as the government, is properly regarded as a crime; because it proves the man capable of it indifferent to all his duties as an Englishman, as a citizen, as a soldier. The spirit of loyalty is far from being lost in Western countries; it has only changed in character, and it is likely to strengthen as time goes on.

Broad tolerance in the matter of beliefs is necessarily a part of the new ethics. It is quite impossible in the present state of mankind that all persons should be well educated, or that the great masses of a nation should attain to the higher forms of culture. For the uneducated a rational system of ethics must long remain out of the question; and it is proper that they should cling to the old emotional forms of moral teaching. The observation of Huxley that he would like to see every unbeliever who could not get a reason for his unbelief publicly put to shame, was an observation of sound common sense. It is only those whose knowledge obliges them to see things from another standpoint than that of the masses who can safely claim to base their rule of life upon philosophical morality. The value of the philosophical morality happens to be only in those directions where it recognizes and supports the truth taught by common morality, which, after all, is the safest guide. Therefore the philosophical moralist will never mock or oppose a belief which he knows to exercise a good influence upon human conduct. He will recognize even the value of many superstitions as being very great; and he will understand that any attempt to suddenly change the beliefs of man in any ethical direction must be mischievous. Such changes as he might desire will come; but they should come gradually and gently, in exact proportion to the expanding capacity of the national mind. Recognizing this probability, several Western countries, notably America, have attempted to introduce into education an entirely new system of ethical teaching—ethical teaching in the broadest sense, and in harmony with the new philosophy. But the result there and elsewhere can only be that which I have said at the beginning of this lecture,—namely, the enlargement of the old moral ideas, and the deeper comprehension of their value in all relations of life.

CHAPTER X

ONE of the great defects of English books printed in the last century is the want of an index. The importance of being able to refer at once to any subject treated of in a book was not recognized until the days when exact scholarship necessitated indexing of the most elaborate kind. But even now we constantly find good books severely criticized because of this deficiency. All that I have said tends to show that even to-day in Western countries the immense importance of systematic arrangement in literary collections is not sufficiently recognized. We have, of course, a great many English anthologies,—that is to say, collections of the best typical compositions of a certain epoch in poetry or in prose. But you must have observed that, in Western countries, nearly all such anthologies are compiled chronologically— not according to the subject of the poems. To this general rule there are indeed a few exceptions. There is a collection of love poetry by Watson, which is famous; a collection of child poetry by Patmore; a collection of "society verse" by Locker-Lampson; and several things of that sort.

But even here the arrangement is not of a special kind; nor is it ever divided according to the subject of each particular poem. I know that some books have been published of late years with such titles as "Poems of the Sea," "Poems of Nature" —but these are of no literary importance at all, and they are not compiled by competent critics. Besides, the subject-heads are always of much too general a kind. The French are far in advance of the English in the art of making anthologies; but even in such splendid anthologies as those of Crépet and of Lemerre the arrangement is of the most general kind,—chronological, and little more.

I was reminded to tell you this, because of several questions recently asked me, which I found it impossible to answer. Many a Japanese student might suppose that Western poetry has its classified arrangements corresponding in some sort to those of Japanese poetry. Perhaps the Germans have something of the kind, but the English and French have not. Any authority upon the subject of Japanese literature can, I have been told, inform himself almost immediately as to all that has been written in poetry upon a particular subject. Japanese poetry has been classified and sub-classified and double-indexed or even quadruple-indexed after a manner incomparably more exact than anything English anthologies can show. I am aware that this fact is chiefly owing to the ancient rules about subjects, seasons, contrasts, and harmonies, after which the old poets used to write. But whatever be said about such rules, there can be no doubt at all of the excellence of the arrangements which the rules produced. It is greatly to be regretted that we have not in English a system of arrangement enabling the student to discover quickly all that has been written upon a particular subject—such as roses, for example, or pine trees, or doves, or the beauties of the autumn season. There is nobody to tell you where to find such things; and as the whole range of English poetry is so great that it takes a great many years even to glance through it, a memorized knowledge of the subjects is impossible for the average man. I believe that Macaulay would have been able to remember almost any reference in the poetry then accessible to scholars,—just as the wonderful Greek scholar Porson could remember the exact place of any text in the whole of Greek literature, and even all the variations of that text. But such men are born only once in hundreds of years; the common memory can not attempt to emulate their feats. And it is very difficult at the present time for the ordinary student of poetry to tell you just how much has been written upon any particular subject by the best English poets.

Now you will recognize some difficulties in the way of a lecturer in attempting to make classifications of English poetry after the same manner that Japanese classification can be made of Japanese poetry. One must read enormously merely to obtain one's materials, and even then the result is not to be thought of as exhaustive. I am going to try to give you a few lectures upon English poetry thus classified, but we must not expect that the lectures will be authoritatively complete. Indeed, we have no time for lectures of so thorough a sort. All that I can attempt will be to give you an idea of the best things that English poets have thought and expressed upon certain subjects.

You know that the old Greeks wrote a great deal of beautiful poetry about insects,—especially about musical insects, crickets, cicadæ, and other insects such as those the Japanese poets have been writing about for so many hundreds of years. But in modern Western poetry there is very little, comparatively speaking, about insects. The English poets have all written a great deal about birds, and especially about singing birds; but very little has been written upon the subject of insects—singing insects. One reason is probably that the number of musical insects in England is very small, perhaps owing to the climate. American poets have written more about insects than English poets have done, though their work is of a much less finished kind. But this is because musical insects in America are very numerous. On the whole, we may say that neither in English ncr in French poetry will you find much about the voices of crickets, locusts, or cicadæ. I could not even give you a special lecture upon that subject. We must take the subject "insect" in a rather general signification; and if we do that we can edit together a nice little collection of poetical examples.

The butterfly was regarded by the Greeks especially as the emblem of the soul and therefore of immortality. We have several Greek remains, picturing the butterfly as perched upon a skull, thus symbolizing life beyond death. And the metamorphosis of the insect is, you know, very often referred to in Greek philosophy. We might expect that English poets would have considered the butterfly especially from this point of view; and we do have a few examples. Perhaps the best known is that of Coleridge.

> The butterfly the ancient Grecians made
> The soul's fair emblem, and its only name—
> But of the soul, escaped the slavish trade
> Of earthly life! For in this mortal frame
> Ours is the reptile's lot, much toil, much blame,
> Manifold motions making little speed,
> And to deform and kill the things whereon we feed.

The allusion to the "name" is of course to the Greek word, *psyche,* which signifies both soul and butterfly. Psyche, as the soul, was pictured by the Greeks as a beautiful girl, with a somewhat sad face, and butterfly wings springing from her shoulders. Coleridge tells us here that although the Greeks likened the soul to the butterfly, we must remember what the butterfly really is,—the last and highest state of insect-being—"escaped the slavish trade of earthly life." What is this so-called slavish trade? It is the necessity of working and struggling in order to live—in order to obtain food. The butterfly is not much of an eater; some varieties, indeed, do not eat at all. All the necessity for eating ended with the life of the larva. In the same manner religion teaches that the soul represents the changed state of man. In this life a man is only like a caterpillar; death changes him into a chrysalis, and out of the chrysalis issues the winged soul which does not have to trouble itself about such matters as eating and drinking. By the word "reptile" in this verse, you must understand caterpillar. Therefore the poet speaks of all our human work as manifold motions making little speed; you have seen how many motions a caterpillar must make in order to go even a little distance, and you must have noticed the manner in which it spoils the appearance of the plant upon which it feeds. There is here an allusion to the strange and terrible fact, that all life—and particularly the life of man—is maintained only by the destruction of other life. In order to live we must kill—perhaps only plants, but in any case we must kill.

Wordsworth has several poems on butterflies, but only one of them is really fine. It is fine, not because it suggests any deep problem, but because

with absolute simplicity it pictures the charming
difference of character in a little boy and a little
girl playing together in the fields. The poem is
addressed to the butterfly.

> Stay near me—do not take thy flight!
> A little longer stay in sight!
> Much converse do I find in thee,
> Historian of my infancy!
> Float near me; do not yet depart!
> Dead times revive in thee:
> Thou bring'st, gay creature as thou art!
> A solemn image to my heart,
>   My father's family.
>
> Oh! pleasant, pleasant were the days,
> The time, when, in our childish plays,
> My sister Emmeline and I
> Together chased the butterfly!
> A very hunter did I rush
> Upon the prey: with leaps and springs
> I followed on from brake to bush;
> But she, God love her, feared to brush
> The dust from off its wings.

What we call and what looks like dust on the
wings of a butterfly, English children are now
taught to know as really beautiful scales or feath-
erlets, but in Wordsworth's time the real structure of the insect was not so well known as now
to little people. Therefore to the boy the coloured matter brushed from the wings would only
have seemed so much dust. But the little girl,

with the instinctive tenderness of the future
mother-soul in her, dreads to touch those strangely
delicate wings; she fears, not only to spoil, but
also to hurt.

Deeper thoughts than memory may still be suggested to English poets by the sight of a butterfly,
and probably will be for hundreds of years to
come. Perhaps the best poem of a half-metaphor-
ical, half-philosophical thought about butterflies
is the beautiful prologue to Browning's "Fifine at
the Fair," which prologue is curiously entitled
"Amphibian"—implying that we are about to
have a reference to creatures capable of living in
two distinctive elements, yet absolutely belonging
neither to the one nor to the other. The poet
swims out far into the sea on a beautiful day; and,
suddenly, looking up, perceives a beautiful butterfly flying over his head, as if watching him. The
sight of the insect at once suggests to him its relation to Greek fancy as a name for the soul; then
he begins to wonder whether it might not really
be the soul, or be the symbol of the soul, of a dead
woman who loved him. From that point of the
poem begins a little metaphysical fantasy about
the possible condition of souls.

> The fancy I had to-day,
> Fancy which turned a fear!
> I swam far out in the bay,
> Since waves laughed warm and clear.

I lay and looked at the sun,
The noon-sun looked at me:
Between us two, no one
Live creature, that I could see.

Yes! There came floating by
Me, who lay floating too,
Such a strange butterfly!
Creature as dear as new:

Because the membraned wings
So wonderful, so wide,
So sun-suffused, were things
Like soul and nought beside.

So much for the conditions of the poet's revery.
He is swimming in the sea; above his face, only a
few inches away, the beautiful butterfly is hover-
ing. Its apparition makes him think of many
things—perhaps first about the dangerous position of the butterfly, for if it should only touch
the water, it is certain to be drowned. But it does
not touch the water; and he begins to think how
clumsy is the man who moves in water compared
with the insect that moves in air, and how ugly
a man is by comparison with the exquisite creature which the Greeks likened to the soul or ghost
of the man. Thinking about ghosts leads him at
once to the memory of a certain very dear ghost
about which he forthwith begins to dream.

What if a certain soul
Which early slipped its sheath,

And has for its home the whole
Of heaven, thus look beneath,

Thus watch one who, in the world,
Both lives and likes life's way,
Nor wishes the wings unfurled
That sleep in the worm, they say?

But sometimes when the weather
Is blue, and warm waves tempt
To free oneself of tether,
And try a life exempt

From worldly noise and dust,
In the sphere which overbrims
With passion and thought,—why, just
Unable to fly, one swims!

This is better understood by paraphrase: "I
wonder if the soul of a certain person, who lately
died, slipped so gently out of the hard sheath of
the perishable body—I wonder if she does not
look down from her home in the sky upon me,
just as that little butterfly is doing at this moment. And I wonder if she laughs at the clumsi-
ness of this poor swimmer, who finds it so much
labour even to move through the water, while she
can move through whatever she pleases by the
simple act of wishing. And this man, strangely
enough, does not want to die, and to become a
ghost. He likes to live very much; he does not
yet desire those soul-wings which are supposed to

be growing within the shell of his body, just as the wings of the butterfly begin to grow in the chrysalis. He does not want to die at all. But sometimes he wants to get away from the struggle and the dust of the city, and to be alone with nature; and then, in order to be perfectly alone, he swims. He would like to fly much better; but he can not. However, swimming is very much like flying, only the element of water is thicker than air."

However, more than the poet's words is suggested here. We are really told that what a fine mind desires is spiritual life, pure intellectual life —free from all the trammels of bodily necessity. Is not the swimmer really a symbol of the superior mind in its present condition? Your best swimmer can not live under the water, neither can he rise into the beautiful blue air. He can only keep his head in the air; his body must remain in the grosser element. Well, a great thinker and poet is ever thus—floating between the universe of spirit and the universe of matter. By his mind he belongs to the region of pure mind,—the ethereal state; but the hard necessity of living keeps him down in the world of sense and grossness and struggle. On the other hand the butterfly, freely moving in a finer element, better represents the state of spirit or soul.

What is the use of being dissatisfied with nature? The best we can do is to enjoy in the im-

agination those things which it is not possible for
us to enjoy in fact.

> Emancipate through passion
> And thought, with sea for sky,
> We substitute, in a fashion,
> For heaven—poetry:

> Which sea, to all intent,
> Gives flesh such noon-disport,
> As a finer element
> Affords the spirit-sort.

Now you see where the poet's vision of a beautiful butterfly has been leading his imagination.
The nearest approach which we can make to the
act of flying, in the body, is the act of swimming.
The nearest approach that we can make to the
heavenly condition, mentally, is in poetry. Poetry,
imagination, the pleasure of emotional expression
—these represent our nearest approach to paradise. Poetry is the sea in which the soul of man
can swim even as butterflies can swim in the air,
or happy ghosts swim in the finer element of the
infinite ether. The last three stanzas of the poem
are very suggestive:

> And meantime, yonder streak
> Meets the horizon's verge;
> That is the land, to seek
> If we tire or dread the surge:

Land the solid and safe—
To welcome again (confess!)
When, high and dry, we chafe
The body, and don the dress.

Does she look, pity, wonder
At one who mimics flight,
Swims—heaven above, sea under,
Yet always earth in sight?

"Streak," meaning an indistinct line, here refers to the coast far away, as it appears to the swimmer. It is just such a word as a good Japanese painter ought to appreciate in such a relation. In suggesting that the swimmer is glad to return to shore again and get warm, the poet is telling us that however much we may talk about the happiness of spirits in heaven—however much we may praise heaven in poetry—the truth is that we are very fond of this world, we like comfort, we like company, we like human love and human pleasures. There is a good deal of nonsense in pretending that we think heaven is a better place than the world to which we belong. Perhaps it is a better place, but, as a matter of fact, we do not know anything about it; and we should be frightened if we could go beyond a certain distance from the real world which we do know. As he tells us this, the poet begins again to think about the spirit of the dead woman. Is she happy? Is she looking at him—and pitying him as he swims, taking good care not to go too far away from the land? Or is she laughing at him, because in his secret thoughts he confesses that he likes to live—that he does not want to become a pure ghost at the present time?

Evidently a butterfly was quite enough, not only to make Browning's mind think very seriously, but to make that mind teach us the truth and seriousness which may attach to very small things—incidents, happenings of daily life, in any hour and place. I believe that is the greatest English poem we have on the subject of the butterfly.

The idea that a butterfly might be, not merely the symbol of the soul, but in very fact the spirit of a dead person, is somewhat foreign to English thought; and whatever exists in poetry on the subject must necessarily be quite new. The idea of a relation between insects, birds, or other living creatures, and the spirits of the dead, is enormously old in Oriental literature;—we find it in Sanskrit texts thousands of years ago. But the Western mind has not been accustomed to think of spiritual life as outside of man; and much of natural poetry has consequently remained undeveloped in Western countries. A strange little poem, "The White Moth," is an exception to the general rule that I have indicated; but I am almost certain that its author, A. T. Quiller-Couch, must have read Oriental books, or obtained his fancy from some Eastern source. As the knowledge of

Indian literature becomes more general in England, we may expect to find poetry much influenced by Oriental ideas. At the present time, such a composition as this is quite a strange anomaly.

> *If a leaf rustled, she would start:*
> *And yet she died, a year ago.*
> *How had so frail a thing the heart*
> *To journey where she trembled so?*
> *And do they turn and turn in fright,*
> *Those little feet, in so much night?*

The light above the poet's head
Streamed on the page and on the cloth,
And twice and thrice there buffeted
On the black pane a white-winged moth:
'Twas Annie's soul that beat outside,
And " Open, open, open! " cried:

" I could not find the way to God;
There were too many flaming suns
For signposts, and the fearful road
Led over wastes where millions
Of tangled comets hissed and burned—
I was bewildered and I turned.

" Oh, it was easy then! I knew
Your window and no star beside.
Look up and take me back to you! "
—He rose and thrust the window wide.
'Twas but because his brain was hot
With rhyming; for he heard her not.

> But poets polishing a phrase
> Show anger over trivial things;
> And as she blundered in the blaze
> Towards him, on ecstatic wings,
> He raised a hand and smote her dead;
> Then wrote *" That I had died instead! "*

The lover, or bereaved husband, is writing a poem of which a part is given in the first stanza—which is therefore put in italics. The action proper begins with the second stanza. The soul of the dead woman taps at the window in the shape of a night-butterfly or moth—imagining, perhaps, that she has still a voice and can make herself heard by the man that she loves. She tells the story of her wandering in space—privileged to pass to heaven, yet afraid of the journey. Now the subject of the poem which the lover happens to be writing inside the room is a memory of the dead woman—mourning for her, describing her in exquisite ways. He can not hear her at all; he does not hear even the beating of the little wings at the window, but he stands up and opens the window—because he happens to feel hot and tired. The moth thinks that he has heard her, that he knows; and she flies toward him in great delight. But he, thinking that it is only a troublesome insect, kills her with a blow of his hand; and then sits down to continue his poem with the words, "Oh, how I wish I could have died instead of that dear woman!" Altogether this is a queer poem in English literature, and I believe almost alone of its kind. But it is queer only because of its rarity of subject. As for construction, it is very good indeed.

I do not know that it is necessary to quote any more poems upon butterflies or moths. There are several others; but the workmanship and the thought are not good enough or original enough to justify their use here as class texts. So I shall now turn to the subject of dragon-flies. Here we must again be very brief. References to dragon-flies are common throughout English poetry, but the references signify little more than a mere colourless mention of the passing of the insect. However, it so happens that the finest modern lines of pure description written about any insect, are about dragon-flies. And they also happen to be by Tennyson. Naturalists and men of science have greatly praised these lines, because of their truth to nature and the accuracy of observation which they show. You will find them in the poem entitled "The Two Voices."

> To-day I saw the dragon-fly
> Come from the wells where he did lie.
>
> An inner impulse rent the veil
> Of his old husk; from head to tail
> Came out clear plates of sapphire mail.

He dried his wings; like gauze they grew;
Thro' crofts and pastures wet with dew
A living rush of light he flew.

There are very few real poems, however, upon
the dragon-fly in English, and considering the extraordinary beauty and grace of the insect, this
may appear strange to you.   But I think that you
can explain the strangeness at a later time.   The
silence of English poets on the subject of insects
as compared with Japanese poets is due to general causes that we shall consider at the close of
the lecture.

Common flies could scarcely seem to be a subject for poetry—disgusting and annoying creatures as they are.   But there are more poems
about the house-fly than about the dragon-fly.
Last year I quoted for you a remarkable and
rather mystical composition by the poet Blake
about accidentally killing a fly.   Blake represents
his own thoughts about the brevity of human life
which had been aroused by the incident.   It is a
charming little poem; but it does not describe the
fly at all.   I shall not quote it here again, because
we shall have many other things to talk about;
but I shall give you the text of a famous little
composition by Oldys on the same topic.   It has
almost the simplicity of Blake,—and certainly
something of the same kind of philosophy.

Busy, curious, thirsty fly,
Drink with me and drink as I;

Freely welcome to my cup,
Couldst thou sip and sip it up:
Make the most of life you may,
Life is short and wears away.

Both alike are mine and thine
Hastening quick to their decline:
Thine's a summer, mine's no more,
Though repeated to threescore.
Threescore summers, when they're gone,
Will appear as short as one!

The suggestion is that, after all, time is only a
very relative affair in the cosmic order of things.
The life of the man of sixty years is not much
longer than the life of the insect which lives but
a few hours, days, or months. Had Oldys, who
belongs to the eighteenth century, lived in our
own time, he might have been able to write something very much more curious on this subject. It
is now known that time, to the mind of an insect,
must appear immensely longer than it appears to
the mind of a man. It has been calculated that
a mosquito or a gnat moves its wings between four
and five hundred times a second. Now the scientific dissection of such an insect, under the micro-
scope, justifies the opinion that the insect must be
conscious of each beat of the wings—just as a man
feels that he lifts his arm or bends his head every
time that the action is performed. A man can not
even imagine the consciousness of so short an interval of time as the five-hundredth part of one

second. But insect consciousness can be aware of
such intervals; and a single day of life might well
appear to the gnat as long as the period of a
month to a man. Indeed, we have reason to suppose that to even the shortest-lived insect life does
not appear short at all; and that the ephemera
may actually, so far as feeling is concerned, live
as long as a man—although its birth and death
does occur between the rising and the setting of
the sun.

We might suppose that bees would form a favourite subject of poetry, especially in countries
where agriculture is practised upon such a scale as
in England. But such is not really the case.
Nearly every English poet makes some reference
to bees, as Tennyson does in the famous couplet—

> The moan of doves in immemorial elms,
> And murmuring of innumerable bees.

But the only really remarkable poem addressed
to a bee is by the American philosopher Emerson.
The poem in question can not be compared as to
mere workmanship with some others which I have
cited; but as to thinking, it is very interesting, and
you must remember that the philosopher who
writes poetry should be judged for his thought
rather than for the measure of his verse. The
whole is not equally good, nor is it short enough
to quote entire; I shall only give the best parts.

Burly, dozing humble-bee,
Where thou art is clime for me.

. . . . .

Zigzag steerer, desert cheerer,
Let me chase thy waving lines;
Keep me nearer, me thy hearer,
Singing over shrubs and vines.

Insect lover of the sun,
Joy of thy dominion!
Sailor of the atmosphere;
Swimmer through the waves of air;
Voyager of light and noon;
Epicurean of June;
Wait, I prithee, till I come
Within earshot of thy hum,—
All without is martyrdom.

. . . . .

Thou, in sunny solitudes,
Rover of the underwoods,
The green silence dost displace
With thy mellow, breezy bass.

. . . . .

Aught unsavory or unclean
Hath my insect never seen;

. . . . .

Wiser far than human seer,
Yellow-breeched philosopher!
Seeing only what is fair,
Sipping only what is sweet,
Thou dost mock at fate and care,
Leave the chaff, and take the wheat.

This is really the poetry of the bee—visiting
only beautiful flowers, and sucking from them
their perfumed juices—always healthy, happy,
and surrounded by beautiful things. A great
rover, a constant wanderer is the bee—visiting
many different places, seeing many different things, but stopping only to enjoy what
is beautiful to the sight and sweet to the
taste. Now Emerson tells us that a wise man
should act like the bee—never stopping to
look at what. is bad, or what is morally ugly,
but seeking only what is beautiful and nourishing
for the mind. It is a very fine thought; and the
manner of expressing it is greatly helped by Emerson's use of curious and forcible words—such as
"burly," "zigzag," and the famous expression
"yellow-breeched philosopher"—which has passed
almost into an American household phrase. The
allusion of course is to the thighs of the bee, covered with the yellow pollen of flowers so as to
make them seem covered with yellow breeches, or
trousers reaching only to the knees.

I do not of course include in the lecture such
child songs about insects as that famous one beginning with the words, "How doth the little busy
bee improve each shining hour." This is no doubt
didactically very good; but I wish to offer you
only examples of really fine poetry on the topic.
Therefore leaving the subject of bees for the
time, let us turn to the subject of musical insects

—the singers of the fields and woods—grasshoppers and crickets.

In Japanese poetry there are thousands of verses upon such insects. Therefore it seems very strange that we have scarcely anything on the subject in English. And the little that we do have is best represented by the poem of Keats on the night cricket. The reference is probably to what we call in England the hearth cricket, an insect which hides in houses, making itself at home in some chink of the brickwork or stonework about a fireplace, for it loves the warmth. I suppose that the small number of poems in English about crickets can be partly explained by the scarcity of night singers. Only the house cricket seems to be very well known. But on the other hand, we can not so well explain the rarity of composition in regard to the day-singers—the grasshoppers and locusts which can be heard, though somewhat faintly, in any English country place after sunset during the warm season. Another queer thing is that the example set by Keats has not been imitated or at least followed even up to the present time.

> The poetry of earth is never dead:
> When all the birds are faint with the hot sun, etc.

In this charming composition you will have noticed the word "stove"; but you must remember that this is not a stove as we understand the term now, and signifies only an old-fashioned fireplace

of brick or tile. In Keats's day there were no iron
stoves. Another word which I want to notice is
the word "poetry" in the first line. By the poetry
of nature the poet means the voices of nature—
the musical sounds made by its idle life in woods
and fields. So the word "poetry" here has especially the meaning of song, and corresponds very
closely to the Japanese word which signifies either
poem or song, but perhaps more especially the
latter. The general meaning of the sonnet is that
at no time, either in winter or in summer, is nature
silent. When the birds do not sing, the grasshoppers make music for us; and when the cold has
killed or banished all other life, then the house
cricket begins with its thin sweet song to make us
think of the dead voices of the summer.

There is not much else of note about the grasshopper and the cricket in the works of the great
English poets. But perhaps you do not know that
Tennyson in his youth took up the subject and
made a long poem upon the grasshopper, but suppressed it after the edition of 1842. He did not
think it good enough to rank with his other work.
But a few months ago the poems which Tennyson
suppressed in the final edition of his works have
been published and carefully edited by an eminent
scholar, and among these poems we find "The
Grasshopper." I will quote some of this poem,
because it is beautiful, and because the fact of its
suppression will serve to show you how very exact

and careful Tennyson was to preserve only the
very best things that he wrote.

> Voice of the summer wind,
> Joy of the summer plain,
> Life of the summer hours,
> Carol clearly, bound along,
> No Tithon thou as poets feign
> (Shame fall 'em, they are deaf and blind),
> But an insect lithe and strong
> Bowing the seeded summer flowers.
> Prove their falsehood and thy quarrel,
> Vaulting on thine airy feet
> Clap thy shielded sides and carol,
> Carol clearly, chirrups sweet.
> Thou art a mailéd warrior in youth and strength
>   complete;
>   Armed cap-à-pie,
>   Full fair to see;
>   Unknowing fear,
>   Undreading loss,
>   A gallant cavalier,
> Sans peur et sans reproche,
>   In sunlight and in shadow,
>   The Bayard of the meadow.

The reference to Tithonus is a reference of
course to a subject afterwards beautifully elaborated in another poem by Tennyson, the great
poem of "Tithonus." The Bayard here referred
to was the great French model of perfect chivalry,
and is sometimes called the last of the feudal
knights. He was said to be without fear and

without blame. You may remember that he was killed by a ball from a gun—it was soon after the use of artillery in war had been introduced; and his dying words were to the effect that he feared there was now an end of great deeds, because men had begun to fight from a distance with machines instead of fighting in the old knightly and noble way with sword and spear. The grasshopper, covered with green plates and bearing so many little sharp spines upon its long limbs, seems to have suggested to Tennyson the idea of a fairy knight in green armour.

As I said before, England is poor in singing insects, while America is rich in them—almost, perhaps, as rich as Japan, although you will not find as many different kinds of singing insects in any one state or district. The singing insects of America are peculiar to particular localities. But the Eastern states have perhaps the most curious insect of this kind. It is called the Katydid. This name is spelt either Katydid, or Catydid—though the former spelling is preferable. Katy, or Katie, is the abbreviation of the name Catherine; very few girls are called by the full name Catherine, also spelt Katherine; because the name is long and unmusical, their friends address them usually as Katy, and their acquaintances, as Kate. Well, the insect of which I am speaking, a kind of *semi,* makes a sound resembling the sound of the words "Katie did!" Hence the name—one of the few

corresponding to the names given to the Japanese
semi, such as *tsuku-tsuku-boshi,* or *minmin-semi.*
The most interesting composition upon this cicada
is by Oliver Wendell Holmes, but it is of the
lighter sort of verse, with a touch of humour in
it. I shall quote a few verses only, as the piece
contains some allusions that would require explanation at considerable length.

> I love to hear thine earnest voice,
>   Wherever thou art hid,
> Thou testy little dogmatist,
>   Thou pretty Katydid!
> Thou mindest me of gentlefolks,—
>   Old gentlefolks are they,—
> Thou say'st an undisputed thing
>   In such a solemn way.

> .   .   .   .   .

> Oh tell me where did Katy live,
>   And what did Katy do?
> And was she very fair and young,
>   And yet so wicked, too?
> Did Katy love a naughty man,
>   Or kiss more cheeks than one?
> I warrant Katy did no more
>   Than many a Kate has done.

> .   .   .   .   .

> Ah, no! The living oak shall crash,
>   That stood for ages still,
> The rock shall rend its mossy base
>   And thunder down the hill,

> Before the little Katydid
> Shall add one word, to tell
> The mystic story of the maid
> Whose name she knows so well.

The word "testy" may be a little unfamiliar to some of you; it is a good old-fashioned English term for "cross," "irritable." The reference to the "old gentlefolks" implies the well-known fact that in argument old persons are inclined to be much more obstinate than young people. And there is also a hint in the poem of the tendency among old ladies to blame the conduct of young girls even more severely than may be necessary. There is nothing else to recommend the poem except its wit and the curiousness of the subject. There are several other verses about the same creature, by different American poets; but none of them is quite so good as the composition of Holmes. However, I may cite a few verses from one of the earlier American poets, Philip Freneau, who flourished in the eighteenth century and the early part of the nineteenth. He long anticipated the fancy of Holmes; but he spells the word Catydid.

> In a branch of willow hid
> Sings the evening Catydid:
> From the lofty locust bough
> Feeding on a drop of dew,
> In her suit of green arrayed
> Hear her singing in the shade—
> Catydid, Catydid, Catydid!

While upon a leaf you tread,
Or repose your little head
On your sheet of shadows laid,
All the day you nothing said;
Half the night your cheery tongue
Revelled out its little song,—
   Nothing else but Catydid.

.   .   .   .   .

Tell me, what did Caty do?
Did she mean to trouble you?
Why was Caty not forbid
To trouble little Catydid?
Wrong, indeed, at you to fling,
Hurting no one while you sing,—
   Catydid! Catydid! Catydid!

To Dr. Holmes the voice of the cicada seemed like the voice of an old obstinate woman, an old prude, accusing a young girl of some fault,—but to Freneau the cry of the little creature seemed rather to be like the cry of a little child complaining—a little girl, perhaps, complaining that somebody had been throwing stones at her, or had hurt her in some way. And, of course, the unfinished character of the phrase allows equally well either supposition.

Before going back to more serious poetry, I want—while we are speaking of American poets —to make one reference to the ironical or satirical poetry which insects have inspired in some minds, taking for example the poem by Charlotte Perkins Stetson about a butterfly. This author is

rather a person of note, being a prominent figure
in educational reforms and the author of a volume
of poems of a remarkably strong kind in the di-
dactic sense.   In other words, she is especially a
moral poet; and unless moral poetry be really very
well executed, it is scarcely worth while classing
it as literature.   I think, however, that the symbolism in the following verses will interest you—
especially when we comment upon them.   The
composition from which they are taken is entitled
"A Conservative."

The poet, walking in the garden one morning,
sees a butterfly, very unhappy, and gifted with
power to express the reason of its unhappiness.
The butterfly says, complaining of its wings,

> " My legs are thin and few
> Where once I had a swarm!
> Soft fuzzy fur—a joy to view—
> Once kept my body warm,
> Before these flapping wing-things grew,
> To hamper and deform! "

> At that outrageous bug I shot
> The fury of mine eye;
> Said I, in scorn all burning hot,
> In rage and anger high,
> " You ignominious idiot!
> Those wings are made to fly! "

> " I do not want to fly," said he,
> " I only want to squirm! "
> 'And he drooped his wings dejectedly,

But still his voice was firm:
" I do not want to be a fly!
I want to be a worm!"

O yesterday of unknown lack!
To-day of unknown bliss!
I left my fool in red and black,
The last I saw was this,—
The creature madly climbing back
Into his chrysalis.

Of course the wings here represent the powers
of the mind—knowledge, reason, will. Men
ought to use these in order to reach still nobler
and higher states of life. But there are men who
refuse to use their best faculties for this end. Such
men are like butterflies who do not want to take
the trouble to fly, but prefer the former condition
of the caterpillar which does nothing but eat and
sleep. As applied to certain forms of conserva-
tism the satire is strong.

Something may now be said as to poems about
spiders. But let me remind you that a spider is
not an insect. Scientifically it has no relation to
the great family of true insects; it belongs to the
very distinct family of the arthropoda or "joint-
footed" animals. But as it is still popularly called
an insect in most European countries, we may be
excused for including it in the subject of the present lecture. I suppose you know that one of the
scientific names for this whole class of creatures
is Arachnida,—a name derived from the Greek

name Arachne. The story of Arachne is interesting, and everybody studying natural history ought to know it. Arachne was a young girl, according to the Greek story, who was very skilful at weaving. She wove cloths of many different colours and beautiful patterns, and everybody admired her work. This made her vain—so vain that at last she said that even the goddess of weaving could not weave better than she. Immediately after she had said that, the terrible goddess herself—Pallas Athena—entered the room. Pallas Athena was not only the goddess of wisdom, you know, but especially the goddess of young girls, presiding over the chastity, the filial piety, and the domestic occupations of virgins; and she was very angry at the conceit of this girl. So she said to her, "You have boasted that you can weave as well as I can; now let me see you weave!" So Arachne was obliged to sit down at her loom and weave in the presence of the goddess; and the goddess also wove, far surpassing the weaving of Arachne. When the weaving was done, the goddess asked the girl, "Now see! which is the better, my work or yours?" And Arachne was obliged to confess that she had been defeated and put to shame. But the goddess was not thoroughly satisfied; to punish Arachne, she touched her lightly with the distaff, saying, "Spin forever!" and thereupon Arachne was changed into a spider, which forever spins and weaves perishable films of per-

ishable shiny thread. Poetically we still may call
a spider Arachne.

I have here a little poem of a touching character entitled "Arachne," by Rose Terry Cooke,
—one of the symbolic poems which are becoming
so numerous in these days of newer and deeper
philosophy. I think that you will like it: a spin-
ster, that is, a maiden passed the age of girlhood,
is the speaker.

> I watch her in the corner there,
> As, restless, bold, and unafraid,
> She slips and floats along the air
> Till all her subtile house is made.
>
> Her home, her bed, her daily food,
> All from that hidden store she draws;
> She fashions it and knows it good,
> By instinct's strong and sacred laws.
>
> No tenuous threads to weave her nest,
> She seeks and gathers there or here;
> But spins it from her faithful breast,
> Renewing still, till leaves are sere.
>
> Then, worn with toil, and tired of life,
> In vain her shining traps are set.
> Her frost hath hushed the insect strife
> And gilded flies her charm forget.
>
> But swinging in the snares she spun,
> She sways to every wintry wind:

Her joy, her toil, her errand done,
Her corse the sport of storms unkind.

The symbolism of these verses will appear to
you more significant when I tell you that it refers
especially to conditions in New England in the
present period. The finest American population
—perhaps the finest Anglo-Saxons ever produced
—were the New Englanders of the early part of
the century. But with the growth of the new century, the men found themselves attracted elsewhere, especially westward; their shrewdness,
their energies, their inventiveness, were needed in
newer regions. And they wandered away by
thousands and thousands, never to come back
again, and leaving the women behind them. Gradually the place of these men was taken by immi-
grants of inferior development—but ` the New
England women had nothing to hope for from
these strangers. The bravest of them also went
away to other states; but myriads who could not
go were condemned by circumstances to stay and
earn their living by hard work without any pros-
pect of happy marriage. The difficulty which a
girl of culture may experience in trying to live by
the work of her hands in New England is something not easily imagined. But it is getting to be
the same in most Western countries. Such a girl
is watching a spider weaving in the corner of the
same room where she herself is weaving; and she
thinks, "Am I not like that spider, obliged to sup-

ply my every need by the work of my own hands, without sympathy, without friends? The spider will spin and catch flies until the autumn comes; then she will die. Perhaps I too must continue to spin until the autumn of my own life—until I become too old to work hard, and die of cold and of exhaustion."

> Poor sister of the spinster clan!
> I too from out my store within
> My daily life and living plan,
> My home, my rest, my pleasure spin.
>
> I know thy heart when heartless hands
> Sweep all that hard-earned web away;
> Destroy its pearled and glittering bands,
> And leave thee homeless by the way.
>
> I know thy peace when all is done.
> Each anchored thread, each tiny knot,
> Soft shining in the autumn sun;
> A sheltered, silent, tranquil lot.
>
> I know what thou hast never known,—
> Sad presage to a soul allowed—
> That not for life I spin, alone,
> But day by day I spin my shroud.

The reference to the sweeping away of the spider's web, of course, implies the pain often caused to such hardworking girls by the meanness of men who employ them only to cheat them—

shopkeepers or manufacturers who take their
work without justly paying for it, and who crit-
icize it as bad in order to force the owner to accept
less money than it is worth. Again a reference
may be intended to the destruction of the home
by some legal trick—some unscrupulous method
of cheating the daughter out of the property be-
queathed to her by her parents.

Notice a few pretty words here. The "pearled"
as applied to the spider's thread gives an intima-
tion of the effect produced by dew on the thread,
but there is also the suggestion of tears upon the
thread work woven by the hands of the girl. The
participle "anchored" is very pretty in its use here
as an adjective, because this word is now especially
used for rope-fastening, whether the rope be steel
or hemp; and particularly for the fastening of the
cables of a bridge. The last stanza might be paraphrased thus: "Sister Spider, I know more than
you—and that knowledge makes me unhappy.
You do not know, when you are spinning your
little web, that you are really weaving your own
shroud. But I know this, my work is slowly but
surely killing me. And I know it because I have
a soul—at least a mind made otherwise than
yours."

The use of the word "soul" in the last stanza
of this poem, brings me back to the question put
forth in an earlier part of the lecture,—why European poets, during the last two thousand years,

have written so little upon the subject of insects? Three thousand, four thousand years ago, the most beautiful Greek poetry—poetry more perfect than anything of English poetry—was written upon insects. In old Japanese literature poems upon insects are to be found by thousands. What is the signification of the great modern silence in Western countries upon this delightful topic? I believe that Christianity, as dogma, accounts for the long silence. The opinions of the early Church refused soul, ghost, intelligence of any sort to other creatures than man. All animals were considered as automata—that is, as self-acting machines, moved by a something called instinct, for want of a better name. To talk about the souls of animals or the spirits of animals would have been very dangerous in the Middle Ages, when the Church had supreme power; it would indeed have been to risk or to invite an accusation of witchcraft, for demons were then thought to take the shape of animals at certain times. To discuss the *mind* of an animal would have been for the Christian faith to throw doubt upon the existence of human souls as taught by the Church; for if you grant that animals are able to think, then you must acknowledge that man is able to think without a soul, or you must acknowledge that the soul is not the essential principle of thought and action. Until after the time of Descartes, who later argued philosophically that animals were only ma-

chines, it was scarcely possible to argue rationally
about the matter in Europe.

Nevertheless, we shall soon perceive that this
explanation will not cover all the facts. You will
naturally ask how it happens that, if the question
be a question of animal souls, birds, horses, dogs,
cats, and many other animals have been made the
subject of Western poems from ancient times.
The silence is only upon the subject of insects.
And, again, Christianity has one saint—the most
beautiful character in all Christian hagiography
—who thought of all nature in a manner that, at
first sight, strangely resembles Buddhism. This
saint was Francis of Assisi, born in the latter
part of the twelfth century, so that he may be said
to belong to the very heart of the Middle Ages,—
the most superstitious epoch of Christianity. Now
this saint used to talk to trees and stones as if they
were animated beings. He addressed the sun as
"my brother sun"; and he spoke of the moon as
his sister. He preached not only to human beings,
but also to the birds and the fishes; and he made
a great many poems on these subjects, full of a
strange and childish beauty. For example, his ser-
mon to the doves, beginning, "My little sisters,
the doves," in which he reminds them that their
form is the emblem or symbol of the Holy Ghost,
is a beautiful poem; and has been, with many
others, translated into nearly all modern languages. But observe that neither St. Francis nor

any other saint has anything to say on the subject of insects.

Perhaps we must go back further than Christianity to guess the meaning of these distinctions. Among the ancient races of Asia, where the Jewish faith arose, there were strange and sinister beliefs about insects—old Assyrian superstitions, old Babylonian beliefs. Insects seemed to those early peoples very mysterious creatures (which they really are) ; and it appears to have been thought that they had a close relation to the world of demons and evil spirits. I suppose you know that the name of one of their gods, Beelzebub, signifies the Lord of Flies. The Jews, as is shown by their Talmudic literature, inherited some of these ideas; and it is quite probable that they were passed on to the days of Christianity. Again, in the early times of Christianity in Northern Africa the Church had to fight against superstitions of an equally strange sort derived from old Egyptian beliefs. Among the Egyptians, certain insects were sacred and became symbols of divinity,— such as the beetle. Now I imagine that for these reasons the subject of insects became at an early time a subject which Christianity thought dangerous, and that thereafter a kind of hostile opinion prevailed regarding any literature upon this topic.

However, to-day things are very different. With the development of scientific studies—especially of microscopic study—it has been found that

insects, far from being the lowliest of creatures,
are the most highly organized of all beings; that
their special senses are incomparably superior to
our own; and that in natural history, from the
evolutional standpoint, they have to be given first
place. This of course renders it impossible any
longer to consider the insect as a trifling subject.
Moreover, the new philosophy is teaching the
thinking classes in all Western countries the great
truth of the unity of life. With the recognition of
such unity, an insect must interest the philosophers
—even the man of ordinary culture—quite as
much as the bird or any other animal.

Nearly all the poems which I have quoted to
you have been poems of very modern date—from
which we may infer that interest in the subject of
insects has been developing of late years only. In
this connection it is interesting to note that a very
religious poet, Whittier, gave us in the last days
of his life a poem upon ants. This would have
seemed strange enough in a former age; it does
not seem strange to-day, and it is beautiful. The
subject is taken from old Jewish literature.

KING SOLOMON AND THE ANTS

Out from Jerusalem
    The King rode with his great
    War chiefs and lords of state,
And Sheba's queen with them;

Comely, but black withal,
   To whom, perchance, belongs
   That wondrous Song of Songs,
Sensuous and mystical,

Whereto devout souls turn
   In fond, ecstatic dream,
   And through its earth-born theme
The Love of Loves discern.

Proud in the Syrian sun,
   In gold and purple sheen,
   The dusky Ethiop queen
Smiled on King Solomon.

Wisest of men, he knew
   The languages of all
   The creatures great or small
That trod the earth or flew.

Across an ant-hill led
   The king's path, and he heard
   Its small folk, and their word
He thus interpreted:

" Here comes the king men greet
   As wise and good and just,
   To crush us in the dust
Under his heedless feet."

The king, understanding the language of insects, turns to the queen and explains to her what
the ants have just said. She advises him to pay no

attention to the sarcasm of the ants—how dare
such vile creatures speak thus about a king! But
Solomon thinks otherwise:

> " Nay," Solomon replied,
> 　" The wise and strong should seek
> 　The welfare of the weak,"
> And turned his horse aside.
>
> His train, with quick alarm,
> 　Curved with their leader round
> 　The ant-hill's peopled mound,
> And left it free from harm.
>
> The jewelled head bent low;
> 　" Oh, king! " she said, " henceforth
> 　The secret of thy worth
> And wisdom well I know.
>
> " Happy must be the State
> 　Whose ruler heedeth more
> 　The murmurs of the poor
> Than flatteries of the great."

The reference to the Song of Songs—also the
Song of Solomon and Canticle of Canticles—may
require a little explanation. The line "Comely
but black withal," is borrowed from a verse of this
song—"I am black but beautiful, oh, ye daughters
of Jerusalem, as the tents of Kedar, as the cur-
tains of Solomon." In another part of the song
the reason of this blackness is given: "I am black,

because the sun hath looked upon me." From which we can see that the word black only means dark, brown, tanned by the sun. Perhaps you do not know that as late as the middle of the eighteenth century it was still the custom in England to speak of a person with black hair and eyes as "a black man"—a custom which Charles Lamb had reason to complain of even at a later day. The tents referred to in the text were probably tents made of camel-skin, such as the Arabs still make, and the colour of these is not black but brown. Whether Solomon wrote the so-called song or not we do not know; but the poet refers to a legend that it was written in praise of the beauty of the dark queen who came from Sheba to visit the wisest man of the world. Such is not, however, the opinion of modern scholars. The composition is really dramatic, although thrown into lyrical form, and as arranged by Renan and others it becomes a beautiful little play, of which each act is a monologue. "Sensuous" the poet correctly calls it; for it is a form of praise of woman's beauty in all its details, as appears in such famous verses as these: "How beautiful are thy feet in shoes, O prince's daughter; the joints of thy thighs are like jewels, the work of the hands of a cunning workman. Thy two breasts are like two young roes that are twins which feed among the lilies." But Christianity, instead of dismissing this part of the Bible, interpreted the song mystically—insisting that the woman described meant the Church, and the lover, Christ. Of course only very pious people continue to believe this; even the good Whittier preferred the legend that it was written about the Queen of Sheba.

I suppose that I ought to end this lecture upon insect poetry by some quotation to which a moral or philosophical meaning can be attached. I shall end it therefore with a quotation from the poet Gray. The poetry of insects may be said to have first appeared in English literature during the second half of the eighteenth century, so that it is only, at the most, one hundred and fifty years old. But the first really fine poem of the eighteenth century relating to the subject is quite as good as anything since composed by Englishmen upon insect life in general. Perhaps Gray referred especially to what we call May-flies—those delicate ghostly insects which hover above water surfaces in fine weather, but which die on the same day that they are born. He does not specify May-flies, however, and we may consider the moral of the poem quite apart from any particular kind of insect. You will find this reference in the piece entitled "Ode on the Spring," in the third, fourth, and fifth stanzas.

> Still is the toiling hand of care:
>   The panting herds repose:
> Yet hark, how through the peopled air
>   The busy murmur glows!

The insect youth are on the wing,
Eager to taste the honied spring,
And float amid the liquid noon:
Some lightly o'er the current skim,
Some show their gaily-gilded trim
    Quick-glancing to the sun.

To Contemplation's sober eye
    Such is the race of man:
And they that creep, and they that fly,
    Shall end where they began.
Alike the Busy and the Gay
But flutter through life's little day,
In fortune's varying colours dressed:
Brushed by the hand of rough Mischance,
Or chilled by Age, their airy dance
    They leave, in dust to rest.

Methinks I hear in accents low
    The sportive kind reply:
Poor moralist! and what art thou?
    A solitary fly!
Thy joys no glittering female meets,
No hive hast thou of hoarded sweets,
No painted plumage to display:
On hasty wings thy youth is flown;
Thy sun is set; thy spring is gone—
    We frolic, while 'tis May.

The poet Gray was never married, and the last
stanza which I have quoted refers jocosely to himself. It is an artistic device to set off the moral
by a little mockery, so that it may not appear too
melancholy.

CHAPTER XI

SOME FRENCH POEMS ABOUT INSECTS

LAST year I gave a lecture on the subject of English poems about insects, with some reference to the old Greek poems on the same subject. But I did not then have an opportunity to make any reference to French poems upon the same subject, and I think that it would be a pity not to give you a few examples.

Just as in the case of English poems about insects, nearly all the French literature upon this subject is new. Insect poetry belongs to the newer and larger age of thought, to the age that begins to perceive the great truth of the unity of life. We no longer find, even in natural histories, the insect treated as a mere machine and unthinking organism; on the contrary its habits, its customs and its manifestation both of intelligence and instinct are being very carefully studied in these times, and a certain sympathy, as well as a certain feeling of respect or admiration, may be found in the scientific treatises of the greatest men who write about insect life. So, naturally, Europe is slowly returning to the poetical standpoint of the old Greeks in this respect. It is not improbable that keeping caged insects as pets may again become a Western custom, as it was in Greek times, when cages were made of rushes or straw for the little creatures. I suppose you have heard that the Japanese custom is very likely to become a fashion in America. If that should really happen, the fact would certainly have an effect upon poetry. I think that it is very likely to happen.

The French poets who have written pretty things about insects are nearly all poets of our own times. Some of them treat the subject from the old Greek standpoint—indeed the beautiful poem of Heredia upon the tomb of a grasshopper is perfectly Greek, and reads almost like a translation from the Greek. Other poets try to express the romance of insects in the form of a monologue, full of the thought of our own age. Others again touch the subject of insects only in connection with the subject of love. I will give one example of each method, keeping the best piece for the last, and beginning with a pretty fancy about a dragonfly.

MA LIBELLULE

En te voyant, toute mignonne,
Blanche dans ta robe d'azure,
Je pensais à quelque madone
Drapée en un peu de ciel pur.

Je songeais à ces belles saintes
Que l'on voyait au temps jadis

Sourire sur les vitres peintes,
Montrant d'un doigt le paradis:

Et j'aurais voulu, loin du monde
Qui passait frivole entre nous,
Dans quelque retraite profonde
T'adorer seul à deux genoux.

This first part of the poem is addressed of course to a beautiful child, some girl between the age of childhood and womanhood:

"Beholding thee, Oh darling one, all white in thy azure dress, I thought of some figure of the Madonna robed in a shred of pure blue sky.

"I dreamed of those beautiful figures of saints whom one used to see in olden times smiling in the stained glass of church windows, and pointing upward to Paradise.

"And I could have wished to adore you alone upon my bended knees in some far hidden retreat, away from the frivolous world that passed between us."

This little bit of ecstasy over the beauty and purity of a child is pretty, but not particularly original. However, it is only an introduction. Now comes the pretty part of the poem:

Soudain un caprice bizarre
Change la scène et le décor,
Et mon esprit au loin s'égare
Sur des grands prés d'azure et d'or.

Où, près de ruisseaux muscules
Gazouillants comme des oiseaux,
Se poursuivent les libellules,
Ces fleurs vivantes des roseaux.

Enfant, n'es tu pas l'une d' elles
Qui me poursuit pour consoler?
Vainement tu caches tes ailes;
Tu marches, mais tu sais voler.

Petite fée au bleu corsage,
Que j'ai connu dès mon berceau,
En revoyant ton doux visage,
Je pense aux joncs de mon ruisseau!

Veux-tu qu'en amoureux fidèles
Nous revenions dans ces prés verts?
Libellule, reprends tes ailes;
Moi, je brulerai tous mes vers!

Et nous irons, sous la lumière,
D'un ciel plus frais et plus léger
Chacun dans sa forme première,
Moi courir, et toi voltiger.

"Suddenly a strange fancy changes for me the scene and the scenery; and my mind wanders far away over great meadows of azure and gold.

"Where, hard by tiny streams that murmur with a sound like voices of little birds, the dragon-flies, those living flowers of the reeds, chase each other at play.

"Child, art thou not one of those dragon-flies, following after me to console me? Ah, it is in vain that thou tryest to hide thy wings; thou dost walk, indeed, but well thou knowest how to fly!

"O little fairy with the blue corsage whom I knew even from the time I was a baby in the cradle; seeing again thy sweet face, I think of the rushes that border the little stream of my native village!

"Dost thou not wish that even now as faithful lovers we return to those green fields? O dragon-fly, take thy wings again, and I—I will burn all my poetry,

"And we shall go back, under the light of the sky more fresh and pure than this, each of us in the original form—I to run about, and thou to hover in the air as of yore."

The sight of a child's face has revived for the poet very suddenly and vividly, the recollection of the village home, the green fields of childhood, the little stream where he used to play with the same little girl, sometimes running after the dragon-fly. And now the queer fancy comes to him that she herself is so like a dragon-fly—so light, graceful, spiritual! Perhaps really she is a dragon-fly following him into the great city, where he struggles to live as a poet, just in order to console him. She hides her wings, but that is only to prevent other people knowing. Why not return once more to the home of childhood, back to the green fields and the sun? "Little dragon-fly," he says to her, "let us go back! do you return to your beautiful summer shape, be a dragon-fly again, expand your wings of gauze; and I shall stop trying to write poetry. I shall burn my verses; I shall go back to the streams where we played as children; I shall run about again with the joy of a child, and with you beautifully flitting hither and thither as a dragon-fly."

Victor Hugo also has a little poem about a dragon-fly, symbolic only, but quite pretty. It is entitled "La Demoiselle"; and the other poem was entitled, as you remember, "Ma Libellule." Both words mean a dragon-fly, but not the same kind of dragon-fly. The French word "demoiselle," which might be adequately rendered into Japanese by the term *ojosan,* refers only to those exquisitely slender, graceful, slow-flitting dragon-flies known to the scientist by the name of Calopteryx. Of course you know the difference by sight, and the reason of the French name will be poetically apparent to you.

> Quand la demoiselle dorée
> S'envole au départ des hivers,
> Souvent sa robe diaprée,
> Souvent son aile est déchirée
> Aux mille dards des buissons **verts.**
>
> Ainsi, jeunesse vive et frêle,
> Qui, t'égarant de tous côtés,

Voles ou ton instinct t'appele,
Souvent tu déchires ton aile
Aux épines des voluptés.

"When, at the departure of winter, the gilded dragon-fly begins to soar, often her many-coloured robe, often her wing, is torn by the thousand thorns of the verdant shrubs.

"Even so, O frail and joyous Youth, who, wandering hither and thither, in every direction, flyest wherever thy instinct calls thee—even so thou dost often tear thy wings upon the thorns of pleasure."

You must understand that pleasure is compared to a rose-bush, whose beautiful and fragrant flowers attract the insects, but whose thorns are dangerous to the visitors. However, Victor Hugo does not use the word for rose-bush, for obvious reasons; nor does he qualify the plants which are said to tear the wings of the dragon-fly. I need hardly tell you that the comparison would not hold good in reference to the attraction of flowers, because dragon-flies do not care in the least about flowers, and if they happen to tear their wings among thorn bushes, it is much more likely to be in their attempt to capture and devour other insects. The merit of the poem is chiefly in its music and colour; as natural history it would not bear criticism. The most beautiful modern French poem about insects, beautiful because of its classical perfection, is I think a sonnet by Heredia, entitled "Épigramme Funéraire"—that is

to say, "Inscription for a Tombstone." This is
an exact imitation of Greek sentiment and expression, carefully studied after the poets of the anthology. Several such Greek poems are extant,
recounting how children mourned for pet insects
which had died in spite of all their care. The
most celebrated one among these I quoted in a
former lecture—the poem about the little Greek
girl Myro who made a tomb for her grasshopper
and cried over it. Heredia has very well copied
the Greek feeling in this fine sonnet:

> Ici gît, Etranger, la verte sauterelle
> Que durant deux saisons nourrit la jeune Hellé,
> Et dont l'aile vibrant sous le pied dentelé.
> Bruissait dans le pin, le cytise, ou l'airelle.
>
> Elle s'est tue, hélas! la lyre naturelle,
> La muse des guérets, des sillons et du blé;
> De peur que son léger sommeil ne soit troublé,
> Ah, passe vite, ami, ne pèse point sur elle.
>
> C'est là. Blanche, au milieu d'une touffe de thym,
> Sa pierre funéraire est fraîchement posée.
> Que d'hommes n'ont pas eu ce suprême destin!
>
> Des larmes d'un enfant la tombe est arrosée,
> Et l'Aurore pieuse y fait chaque matin
> Une libation de gouttes de rosée.

"Stranger, here reposes the green grasshopper
that the young girl Helle cared for during two

seasons,—the grasshopper whose wings, vibrating under the strokes of its serrated feet, used to resound in the pine, the trefoil and the whortleberry.

"She is silent now, alas! that natural lyre, muse of the unsown fields, of the furrows, and of the wheat. Lest her light sleep should be disturbed, ah! pass quickly, friend! do not be heavy upon her.

"It is there. All white, in the midst of a tuft of thyme, her funeral monument is placed, in cool shadow; how many men have not been able to have this supremely happy end!

"By the tears of a child the insect's tomb is watered; and the pious goddess of dawn each morning there makes a libation of drops of dew."

This reads very imperfectly in a hasty translation; the original charm is due to the perfect art of the form. But the whole thing, as I have said before, is really Greek, and based upon a close study of several little Greek poems on the same kind of subject. Little Greek girls thousands of years ago used to keep singing insects as pets, every day feeding them with slices of leek and with fresh water, putting in their little cages sprigs of the plants which they liked. The sorrow of the child for the inevitable death of her insect pets at the approach of winter, seems to have inspired many Greek poets. With all tenderness, the child would make a small grave for the insect, bury it solemnly, and put a little white stone above the place to imitate a grave-stone. But of course she would want an inscription for this tombstone—perhaps would ask some of her grown-up friends to compose one for her. Sometimes the grown-up friend might be a poet, in which case he would compose an epitaph for all time.

I suppose you perceive that the solemnity of this imitation of the Greek poems on the subject is only a tender mockery, a playful sympathy with the real grief of the child. The expression, "pass, friend," is often found in Greek funeral inscriptions together with the injunction to tread lightly upon the dust of the dead. There is one French word to which I will call attention,—the word "guérets." We have no English equivalent for this term, said to be a corruption of the Latin word "veractum," and meaning fields which have been ploughed but not sown.

Not to dwell longer upon the phase of art indicated by this poem, I may turn to the subject of crickets. There are many French poems about crickets. One by Lamartine is known to almost every French child.

> Grillon solitaire,
> Ici comme moi,
> Voix qui sors de terre,
> Ah! réveille-toi!
> J'attise la flamme,
> C'est pour t'égayer;
> Mais il manque une âme,
> Une âme au foyer.

Grillon solitaire,
Voix qui sors de terre,
Ah! réveille-toi
  Pour moi.

Quand j'étais petite
Comme ce berceau,
Et que Marguerite
Filait son fuseau,
Quand le vent d'automne
Faisait tout gémir,
Ton cri monotone
M'aidait à dormir.

Grillon solitaire,
Voix qui sors de terre,
Ah! réveille-toi
  Pour moi.

Seize fois l'année
A compté mes jours;
Dans la cheminée
Tu niches toujours.
Je t'écoute encore
Aux froides saisons.
Souvenir sonore
Des vieilles maisons.

Grillon solitaire,
Voix qui sors de terre,
Ah! réveille-toi
  Pour moi.

It is a young girl who thus addresses the cricket

of the hearth, the house cricket. It is very common in country houses in Europe. This is what she says:

"Little solitary cricket, all alone here just like myself, little voice that comes up out of the ground, ah, awake for my sake! I am stirring up the fires, that is just to make you comfortable; but there lacks a presence by the hearth; a soul to keep me company.

"When I was a very little girl, as little as that cradle in the corner of the room, then, while Margaret our servant sat there spinning, and while the autumn wind made everything moan outside, your monotonous cry used to help me to fall asleep.

"Solitary cricket, voice that issues from the ground, awaken, for my sake.

"Now I am sixteen years of age and you are still nestling in the chimneys as of old. I can hear you still in the cold season,—like a sound—memory,—a sonorous memory of old houses.

"Solitary cricket, voice that issues from the ground, awaken, O awaken for my sake."

I do not think this pretty little song needs any explanation; I would only call your attention to the natural truth of the fancy and the feeling. Sitting alone by the fire in the night, the maiden wants to hear the cricket sing, because it makes her think of her childhood, and she finds happiness in remembering it.

So far as mere art goes, the poem of Gautier on the cricket is very much finer than the poem of Lamartine, though not so natural and pleasing. But as Gautier was the greatest master of French verse in the nineteenth century, not excepting Victor Hugo, I think that one example of his poetry on insects may be of interest. He was very poor, compared with Victor Hugo; and he had to make his living by writing for newspapers, so that he had no time to become the great poet that nature intended him to be. However, he did find time to produce one volume of highly finished poetry, which is probably the most perfect verse of the nineteenth century, if not the most perfect verse ever made by a French poet; I mean the "Emaux et Camées." But the little poem which I am going to read to you is not from the "Émaux et Camées."

Souffle, bise! Tombe à flots, pluie!
Dans mon palais tout noir de suie,
Je ris de la pluie et du vent;
En attendant que l'hiver fuie,
Je reste au coin du feu, rêvant.

C'est moi qui suis l'esprit de l'âtre!
Le gaz, de sa langue bleuâtre,
Lèche plus doucement le bois;
La fumée en filet d'albâtre,
Monte et se contourne à ma voix.

La bouilloire rit et babille;
La flamme aux pieds d'argent sautille
En accompagnant ma chanson;
La bûche de duvet s'habille;
La sève bout dans le tison.

. . . . .

Pendant la nuit et la journée
Je chante sous la cheminée;
Dans mon langage de grillon
J'ai, des rebuts de son aînée,
Souvent consolé Cendrillon.

. . . . .

Quel plaisir? Prolonger sa veille,
Regarder la flamme vermeille
Prenant à deux bras le tison,
A tous les bruits prêter l'oreille,
Entendre vivre la maison.

Tapi dans sa niche bien chaude,
Sentir l'hiver qui pleure et rôde,
Tout blême, et le nez violet,
Tâchant de s'introduire en fraude
Par quelque fente du volet!

This poem is especially picturesque, and is intended to give us the comfortable sensations of a
winter night by the fire, and the amusement of
watching the wood burn and of hearing the kettle
boiling. You will find that the French has a particular quality of lucid expression; it is full of
clearness and colour.

"Blow on, cold wind! pour down, O rain. I, in

my soot-black palace, laugh at both rain and wind;
and while waiting for winter to pass I remain in
my corner by the fire dreaming.

"It is I that am really the spirit of the hearth!
The gaseous flame licks the wood more softly with
its bluish tongue when it hears me; and the smoke
rises up like an alabaster thread, and curls itself
about (or twists) at the sound of my voice.

"The kettle chuckles and chatters; the golden-
footed flame leaps, dancing to the accompaniment
of my song (or in accompaniment to my song);
the great log covers itself with down, the sap boils
in the wooden embers ("duvet," meaning "down,"
refers to the soft fluffy white ash that forms upon
the surface of burning wood).

"All night and all day I sing below the chim-
ney. Often in my cricket-language, I have con-
soled Cinderella for the snubs of her elder sister.

"Ah, what pleasure to sit up at night, and watch
the crimson flames embracing the wood (or hug-
ging the wood) with both arms at once, and to
listen to all the sounds and to hear the life of
the house!

"Nestling in one's good warm nook, how pleasant to hear Winter, who weeps and prowls round
about the house outside, all wan and blue-nosed
with cold, trying to smuggle itself inside some
chink in the shutter!"

Of course this does not give us much about the
insect itself, which remains invisible in the poem,

just as it really remains invisible in the house where the voice is heard. Rather does the poem express the feelings of the person who hears the cricket.

When we come to the subject of grasshoppers, I think that the French poets have done much better than the English. There are many poems on the field grasshopper; I scarcely know which to quote first. But I think you would be pleased with a little composition by the celebrated French painter, Jules Breton. Like Rossetti he was both painter and poet; and in both arts he took for his subjects by preference things from country life. This little poem is entitled "Les Cigales." The word "cigales," though really identical with our word "cicala," seldom means the same thing. Indeed the French word may mean several different kinds of insects, and it is only by studying the text that we can feel quite sure what sort of insect is meant.

Lorsque dans l'herbe mûre ancun épi ne bouge,
Qu'à l'ardeur des rayons crépite le frement,
Que le coquelicot tombe languissament
Sous le faible fardeau de sa corolle rouge,

Tous les oiseaux de l'air ont fait taire leur chants;
Les ramiers paresseux, au plus noir des ramures,
Somnolents, dans les bois, ont cessé leurs murmures
Loin du soleil muet incendiant les champs.

Dans le blé, cependant, d'intrépides cigales
Jetant leurs mille bruits, fanfare de l'été,
Ont frénétiquement et sans trève agité
Leurs ailes sur l'airaine de leurs folles cymbales.

Trémoussantes, deboutes sur les longs épis d'or,
Virtuoses qui vont s'éteindre avant l'automne,
Elles poussent au ciel leur hymne monotone
Que dans l'ombre des nuits retentisse encore.

Et rien n'arrêtera leurs cris intarissables;
Quand on les chassera de l'avoine et des blés.
Elles émigreront sur les buissons brulés
Qui se meurent de soif dans les deserts de sable.

Sur l'arbuste effeuillé, sur les chardons flétris
Qui laissent s'envoler leur blanche chevelure,
On reverra l'insecte à la forte encolure,
Pleine d'ivresse, toujours s'exalter dans ses cris.

Jusqu'à ce qu'ouvrant l'aile en lambeaux arrachée,
Exasperé, brulant d'un feu toujours plus pur,
Son œil de bronze fixe et tendu vers l'azur,
Il expire en chantant sur la tige séchée.

For the word "encolure" we have no English equivalent; it means the line of the neck and shoulder—sometimes the general appearance or shape of the body.

"When in the ripening grain field not a single ear of wheat moves; when in the beaming heat the corn seems to crackle; when the poppy lan-

guishes and bends down under the feeble burden
of its scarlet corolla,

"Then all the birds of the air have hushed their
songs; even the indolent doves, seeking the dark-
est part of the foliage in the tree, have become
drowsy in the woods, and have ceased their cooing, far from the fields, which the silent sun is
burning.

"Nevertheless, in the wheat, the brave grasshoppers uttering their thousand sounds, a trum-
pet flourish of summer, have continued furiously
and unceasingly to smite their wings upon the
brass of their wild cymbal.

"Quivering as they stand upon the long gold
ears of the grain, master musicians who must die
before the coming of Fall, they sound to heaven
their monotonous hymn, which re-echoes even in
the darkness of the night.

"And nothing will check their inexhaustible
shrilling. When chased away from the oats and
from the wheat, they will migrate to the scorched
bushes which die of thirst in the wastes of
sand.

"Upon the leafless shrubs, upon the dried up
thistles, which let their white hair fall and float
away, there the sturdily-built insect can be seen
again, filled with enthusiasm, even more and more
excited as he cries,

"Until, at last, opening his wings, now rent into
shreds, exasperated, burning more and more

fiercely in the frenzy of his excitement, and with
his eyes of bronze always fixed motionlessly upon
the azure sky, he dies in his song upon the withered grain."

This is difficult to translate at all satisfactorily,
owing to the multitude of images compressed together. But the idea expressed is a fine one—the
courage of the insect challenging the sun, and only
chanting more and more as the heat and the thirst
increase. The poem has, if you like, the fault of
exaggeration, but the colour and music are very
fine; and even the exaggeration itself has the merit
of making the images more vivid.

It will not be necessary to quote another text;
we shall scarcely have the time; but I want to
translate to you something of another poem upon
the same insect by the modern French poet Jean
Aicard. In this poem, as in the little poem by
Gautier, which I quoted to you, the writer puts
his thought in the mouth of the insect, so to say—
that is, makes the insect tell its own story.

"I am the impassive and noble insect that sings
in the summer solstice from the dazzling dawn all
the day long in the fragrant pine-wood. And my
song is always the same, regular as the equal
course of the season and of the sun. I am the
speech of the hot and beaming sun, and when
the reapers, weary of heaping the sheaves together, lie down in the lukewarm shade, and sleep
and pant in the ardour of noonday—then more

than at any other time do I utter freely and joyously that double-echoing strophe with which my whole body vibrates. And when nothing else moves in all the land round about, I palpitate and loudly sound my little drum. Otherwise the sunlight triumphs; and in the whole landscape nothing is heard but my cry,—like the joy of the light itself.

"Like a butterfly I take up from the hearts of the flowers that pure water which the night lets fall into them like tears. I am inspired only by the almighty sun. Socrates listened to me; Virgil made mention of me. I am the insect especially beloved by the poets and by the bards. The ardent sun reflects himself in the globes of my eyes. My ruddy bed, which seems to be powdered like the surface of fine ripe fruit, resembles some exquisite key-board of silver and gold, all quivering with music. My four wings, with their delicate net-work of nerves, allow the bright down upon my black back to be seen through their transparency. And like a star upon the forehead of some divinely inspired poet, three exquisitely mounted rubies glitter upon my head."

These are fair examples of the French manner of treating the interesting subject of insects in poetry. If you should ask me whether the French poets are better than the English, I should answer, "In point of feeling, no." The real value of such examples to the student should be emotional, not descriptive. I think that the Japanese poems on insects, though not comparable in point of mere form with some of the foreign poems which I have quoted, are better in another way— they come nearer to the true essence of poetry. For the Japanese poets have taken the subject of insects chiefly for the purpose of suggesting human emotion; and that is certainly the way in which such a subject should be used. Remember that this is an age in which we are beginning to learn things about insects which could not have been even imagined fifty years ago, and the more that we learn about these miraculous creatures, the more difficult does it become for us to write poetically about their lives, or about their possible ways of thinking and feeling. Probably no mortal man will ever be able to imagine how insects think or feel or hear or even see. Not only are their senses totally different from those of animals, but they appear to have a variety of special senses about which we can not know anything at all. As for their existence, it is full of facts so atrocious and so horrible as to realize most of the imaginations of old about the torments of hell. Now, for these reasons to make an insect speak in poetry—to put one's thoughts, so to speak, into the mouth of an insect—is no longer consistent with poetical good judgment. No; we must think of insects either in relation to the mystery of their marvellous lives, or in relation to the emotion which their sweet and melancholy music makes within our minds. The impressions produced by hearing the shrilling of crickets at night or by hearing the storm of cicadæ in summer woods—those impressions indeed are admirable subjects for poetry, and will continue to be for all time.

When I lectured to you long ago about Greek and English poems on insects, I told you that nearly all the English poems on the subject were quite modern. I still believe that I was right in this statement, as a general assertion; but I have found one quaint poem about a grasshopper, which must have been written about the middle of the seventeenth century or, perhaps, a little earlier. The date of the author's birth and death are respectively 1618 and 1658. His name, I think, you are familiar with—Richard Lovelace, author of many amatory poems, and of one especially famous song, "To Lucasta, on Going to the Wars" —containing the celebrated stanza—

> Yet this inconstancy is such
>   As you too shall adore;
> I could not love thee, Dear, so much,
>   Loved I not honour more.

Well, as I said, this man wrote one pretty little poem on a grasshopper, which antedates most of the English poems on insects, if not all of them.

THE GRASSHOPPER

O Thou that swing'st upon the waving ear
  Of some well-filled oaten beard,
Drunk every night with a delicious tear
  Dropt thee from heaven, where now th'art rear'd!

The joys of earth and air are thine entire,
  That with thy feet and wings dost hop and fly;
And when thy poppy works, thou dost retire
  To thy carved acorn-bed to lie.

Up with the day, the Sun thou welcom'st then,
  Sport'st in the gilt plaits of his beams,
And all these merry days mak'st merry men
  Thyself, and melancholy streams.

A little artificial, this poem written at least two
hundred and fifty years ago; but it is pretty in
spite of its artifice. Some of the conceits are so
quaint that they must be explained. By the term
"oaten beard," the poet means an ear of oats;
and you know that the grain of this plant is furnished with very long hair, so that many poets
have spoken of the bearded oats. You may remember in this connection Tennyson's phrase "the
bearded barley" in the "Lady of Shalott," and
Longfellow's term "bearded grain" in his famous
poem about the Reaper Death. When a person's beard is very thick, we say in England
to-day "a full beard," but in the time of Shakespeare they used to say "a well filled beard"—
hence the phrase in the second line of the first
stanza.

In the third line the term "delicious tear" means dew,—which the Greeks called the tears of the night, and sometimes the tears of the dawn; and the phrase "drunk with dew" is quite Greek—so we may suspect that the author of this poem had been reading the Greek Anthology. In the third line of the second stanza the word "poppy" is used for sleep—a very common simile in Elizabethan times, because from the poppy flower was extracted the opiate which enables sick persons to sleep. The Greek authors spoke of poppy sleep. "And when thy poppy works," means, when the essence of sleep begins to operate upon you, or more simply, when you sleep. Perhaps the phrase about the "carved acorn-bed" may puzzle you; it is borrowed from the fairy-lore of Shakespeare's time, when fairies were said to sleep in little beds carved out of acorn shells; the simile is used only by way of calling the insect a fairy creature. In the second line of the third stanza you may notice the curious expression about the "gilt plaits" of the sun's beams. It was the custom in those days, as it still is in these, for young girls to plait their long hair; and the expression "gilt plaits" only means braided or plaited golden hair. This is perhaps a Greek conceit; for classic poets spoke of the golden hair of the Sun God as illuminating the world. I have said that the poem is a little artificial, but I think you will find it pretty, and even the whimsical similes are "precious" in the best sense.

CHAPTER XII

THE subject of Finnish poetry ought to have a special interest for the Japanese student, if only for the reason that Finnish poetry comes more closely in many respects to Japanese poetry than any other form of Western poetry. Indeed it is supposed that the Finnish race is more akin to the Tartar races, and therefore probably to the Japanese, than the races of Europe proper. Again, through Longfellow, the value of Finnish poetry to English poetry was first suggested, and I think you know that Longfellow's Indian epic, "The Song of Hiawatha," was modelled entirely upon the Finnish "Kalevala."

But a word about the "Kalevala," which has a very interesting history. I believe you know that at the beginning of the nineteenth century, the "Kalevala" was not known to exist. During the first half of the century, Finnish scholars in the University of Helsingfors (where there is now a great and flourishing university) began to take literary interest in the popular songs of Finland. For years the people had been singing extraordinary

228

songs, full of a strange beauty and weirdness quite unlike any other popular songs of Europe; and for centuries professional singers had been wandering about the country teaching these songs to the accompaniment of a kind of *biwa* called Kantela. The scholars of the University began to collect these songs from the mouths of the peasants and musicians—at first with great difficulty, afterwards with much success. The difficulty was a very curious one. In Finland the ancient pagan religion had really never died; the songs of the peasants were full of allusions to the old faith and the old gods, and the orthodox church had often attempted in vain to prevent the singing of these songs, because they were not Christian. So the peasants at first thought that the scholars who wanted to copy the songs were government spies or church spies who wanted evidence to justify punishments. When the fears of the people had been removed and when they came to understand that the questioners were only scholars interested in literary beauty, all the secret stores of songs were generously opened, and an immense collection of oral literature was amassed in the University at Helsingfors.

The greatest of the scholars engaged in the subsequent work of arranging and classifying was Doctor Lönnrot. While examining the manuscript of these poems he was struck by the fact that, put together in a particular order, they nat-

urally made one great continuous story or epic.
Was it possible that the Finnish people had had
during all these centuries an epic unknown to the
world of literature? Many persons would have
ridiculed the idea. But Lönnrot followed up that
idea, and after some years' study he disengaged
from all that mass of song something in the shape
of a wonderful epic, the epic of the "Kalevala."
Lönnrot was probably, almost certainly, the only
one who had even understood the idea of an
epic of this kind. The peasants did not know.
They only had the fragments of the whole;
parts of the poem existed in one province,
parts in another; no Finnish musician had ever
known the whole. The whole may have been
made first by Lönnrot. At all events he was the
Homer of the "Kalevala," and it was fortunate
for Finland that he happened to be himself both
a scholar and a poet—qualifications seldom united
in the same person.

What is the "Kalevala" as we now possess it?
It is an epic, but not like any other epic in the
world, for the subject of it is Magic. We might
call it the Epic of Magic. It is the story of how
the world and the heaven and the sun and the
moon and the stars, the elements and the races of
living creatures and all other things were created
by magic; also how the first inhabitants of the
world lived, and loved, and fought. But there is
another thing to be said in a general way about

this magic. The magic of "Kalevala" is not like
anything else known by that name in European
literature. The magic of "Kalevala" is entirely
the magic of words. These ancient people believed in the existence of words, by the utterance
of which anything might be accomplished. Instead of buying wood and hiring carpenters, you
might build a house by uttering certain magical
words. If you had no horse and wanted to travel
rapidly, you could make a horse for yourself out
of bits of bark and old sticks by uttering over
them certain magical words. But this was not all.
Beings of intellect, men and women, whole armies
of men, in fact, might be created in a moment by
the utterance of these mystical words. There is
the real subject of the "Kalevala."

I told you that the epic is not like anything
else in European literature and not like anything
else in the world as to the subject. But this is
not the case as regards the verse. The verse is
not like Japanese verse, indeed, but it comes
nearer to it than any other European verse does.
Of course even in Finnish verse, accents mean a
great deal, and accent means nothing at all in
Japanese verse. But I imagine something very
much like Finnish verse might be written in Japanese, provided that in reciting it a slight stress
is thrown on certain syllables. Of course you know
something about Longfellow's "Hiawatha"—
such lines as these:

And the evening sun descending
Set the clouds on fire with redness,
Burned the broad sky like a prairie,
Left upon the level water
One long track and trail of splendour,
Down whose stream, as down a river,
Westward, westward Hiawatha
Sailed into the fiery sunset,
Sailed into the purple vapours,
Sailed into the dusk of evening.

You will observe this is verse of eight syllables
with four trochees to a line. Now it is perhaps
as near to Finnish verse as English verse can be
made. But the Finnish verse is more musical, and
it is much more flexible, and the rules of it can
be better carried out than in English. There is
much more to be thought about than the placing
of four trochaic feet to a line. Not only must
the verse be trochaic, it must also be alliterative,
and it must also be, to some extent, rhymed verse
—a matter which Longfellow did not take into
consideration. That would have doubled his difficulty. To make verse trochaic, alliterative and
rhymed, is very difficult indeed—that is, to do it
well. Only one liberty is allowed; it is not necessary that the rhyme shall be regular and constant;
it is necessary only that it should be occasional.
But the interest of Finnish verse does not end
here. I have not yet mentioned the most important law of Finnish poetry—the law of paral-

lelism or repetition. Parallelism is the better
word. It means the repetition of a thought in a
slightly modified way. It is parallelism especially
that makes so splendid the English translation of
the Bible, and the majesty of such passages in the
Book of Common Prayer as the Funeral Service.
So that Finnish poetry is anything but very simple.
We may now sum it up thus—trochaic verse of
eight syllables, with alliteration and rhyme, a
caesura in the same part of every line, and every
line reiterated in parallelism.

A little above I mentioned the English of the
Bible. Long ago I explained why that English is
so beautiful and so strong. But remember that
much of the best of the Bible, in the original Hebrew, was not prose but verse, and that the fine
effects have been produced by translating the verse
into musical prose. The very effect can be produced by translating the "Kalevala" into prose.
Occasionally the passages are of surprising
beauty, and they are always of surprising strangeness.

It is in parallelism especially that Finnish poetry offers a contrast to Japanese, but there is no
reason whatever why, in the longer poems of
Japanese poetry, parallelism could not be used.
All things have value according to place and time,
and this has value—provided that it has a special
effect on a special occasion. All through the "Kalevala," all through five hundred pages, large

pages, the parallelism is carried on, and yet one never gets tired. It is not monotonous. But that is because the subject is so well adapted to this form of poetry. See how the poem opens, when the poet begins to talk about what he is going to sing:

"Anciently my father sang me these words in hewing the handle of his ax; anciently my mother taught me these words as she turned her spindle. In that time I was only a child, a little child at the breast,—a useless little being creeping upon the floor at the feet of its nurse, its cheek bedaubed with milk. And there are other words which I drew from the spring of knowledge, which I found by the wayside, which I snatched from the heart of the thickets, which I detached from the branches of the trees, which I gathered at the edges of the pastures—when, in my infancy, I used to go to guard the flocks, in the midst of the honey-streaming meadows, upon the gold-shining hills, behind the black Murikki, behind the spotted Kimmo, my favourite cows.

"Also the cold sang the songs, the rain sang me verses, the winds of heaven, the waves of the sea made me hear their poems, the birds instructed me with their melodies, the long-haired trees invited me to their concerts. And all the songs I gathered together, I rolled them up in a skin, I carried them away in my beautiful little holiday sledge, I deposited them in the bottom of a chest of brass, upon the highest shelf of my treasure house."

Now when a poem opens that way we may be sure that there are great things in it; and some of these great things we shall read about presently. The "Kalevala" is full of wonderful stories. But in the above quotation, I want you to see how multiple it is, and yet it is beautiful. Now there is a very interesting thing yet to tell you about this parallelism. Such poems as those of the "Kalevala" have always to be sung not by one singer but by two. The two singers straddle a bench facing each other and hold each other's hands. Then they sing alternately, each chanting one line, rocking back and forward, pulling each other to and fro as they sing—so that it is like the motion of rowing. One chants a line and pulls backward, then the other chants the next line and pulls in the opposite direction. Not to be able to answer at once would be considered a great disgrace; and every singer has to be able to improvise as well as to sing. And that is the signification of the following verse:

"Put thy hand to my hand—place thy fingers between my fingers—that we may sing of the things which are."

The most beautiful story in this wonderful book is the story of Kullervo. It was after reading this

story that Longfellow imagined his story of the
Strong Man Kwasind. Kullervo is born so strong
that as an infant he breaks his cradle to pieces,
and as a boy he can not do any work, for all the
tools and instruments break in his grasp. Therefore he gives a great deal of trouble at home and
has to go out into the world to seek his fortune.
In the world, of course, he has just the same trouble; for nobody will employ him very long. However, the story of Kullervo's feats of strength,
though interesting, need not now concern us. The
great charm of this composition is in the description of a mother's love which it contains. Kullervo brought misfortune everywhere simply by
his strength and by his great passions—at last
committing a terrible crime, causing the death of
his own sister, whom he does not recognize. He
goes back home in desperation and remorse; and
there everybody regards him with horror, except
only his mother. She alone tries to console him;
she alone tells him that repentance may bring him
rest. He then proposes to go away and amend
his wrong-doing in solitude. But first he bids them
all goodbye, and the episode is characteristic.

Kullervo, the son of Kalervo, gets him ready
to depart; he goes to his old father and says:
"Farewell now, O my dear father. Wilt thou regret me bitterly, when thou shalt learn that I am
dead?—that I have disappeared from among the
multitude of the living?—that I no longer am

one of the members of thy family?" The father
answered: "No, certainly I will not regret thee
when I shall hear that thou art dead. Another
son perchance will be born to me—a son who will
grow up better and wiser than thou."

Kullervo, son of Kalervo, answered: "And I
also will not be sorry if I hear that thou art dead.
Without any trouble I can find me such a father
as thou—a stone-hearted father, a clay-mouthed
father, a berry-eyed father, a straw-bearded
father, a father whose feet are made of the roots
of the willow tree, a father whose flesh is decay-
ing wood." Why does Kullervo use these extraordinary terms? It is a reference to magic—
out of stone and clay and straw, a phantom man
can be made, and Kullervo means to say that his
father is no more to him than a phantom father,
an unreal father, a father who has no fatherly
feeling. His brothers and sisters all questioned
in turn if they will be sorry to hear that he is dead,
make the same cruel answer; and he replies to
them with the same angry words. But it is very
different when he speaks to his mother.

For to his mother he said—"Oh my sweet
mother, my beautiful nurse, my loved protectress,
wilt thou regret me bitterly when thou shalt learn
that I am dead, that I have disappeared from the
multitude of the living, that I am no longer one
of the members of thy family?"

The mother made answer: "Thou does not

comprehend the soul of the mother—thou canst not understand the heart of the mother. Assuredly will I regret thee most bitterly when I shall learn that thou art dead, that thou hast disappeared from among the multitude of the living, that thou hast ceased to be one of the members of my family. Floods of tears shall I weep in my chamber. The waves of tears will overflow on the floor. And upon the stairway lamentably shall I weep; and in the stable loudly shall I sorrow. Upon the icy ways the snow shall melt under my tears—under my tears the earth of the roads shall melt away; under my tears new meadow grass shall grow up, green sprouting, and through that grass little streams shall murmur away." To this mother, naturally, Kullervo says no unkind words. He goes away, able at least to feel that there is one person in the world who loves him and one person in the world whom he loves. But how much his mother really loves him he does not yet know; he will know that later—it forms the most beautiful part of the poem.

"Kullervo directed his steps once more to the home of his fathers. Desolate he found it, desolate and deserted; no person advanced to salute him, no person came to press his hand, to give him welcome.

"He drew near to the hearth: the embers were extinguished. By that he knew that his mother had ceased to be.

"He drew near to the fire-place, and the stones of the fire-place were cold. By that he knew that his father had ceased to be.

"He turned his eyes upon the floor of his home; the planks of the floor were covered with dirt and rubbish. By that he knew that his sister had ceased to be.

"To the shore of the sea he went; the boat that used to be there was there no longer. By that he knew that his brother had ceased to be.

"Then he began to weep. For a whole day he wept, for two whole days he wept; then he cried aloud: 'O my mother, O my sweet mother, what didst thou leave thy son yet in the world? Alas! now thou canst hear me no longer; and it is in vain that I stand above thy tomb, that I sob over the place of thine eyebrows, over the place of thy temples; it is in vain that I cry out my grief above thy dead forehead.'

"The mother of Kullervo awakened in her tomb, and out of the depth of the dust she spake to him: 'I have left the dog Mastif, in order that thou mayst go with him to the chase. Take therefore the faithful dog, and go with him into the wild forest, into the dark wilderness, even to the dwelling place, far away, of the blue-robed Virgins of the wood, and there thou wilt seek thy nourishment, thou wilt ask for the game that is necessary to thy existence.' "

It was believed that there was a particular forest god, who protected the trees and the wild things of the wood. The hunter could be successful in the chase only upon condition of obtaining his favour and permission to hunt. This explains the reference to the abode of the forest god. But Kullervo can not go far; his remorse takes him by the throat.

"Kullervo, son of Kalervo, took his faithful dog, and directed his steps toward the wild forest, toward the dark wilderness. But when he had gone only a little way he found himself at the very place where he had outraged the young girl, where he had dishonoured the child of his mother. And all things there mourned for her—all things; the soft grass and the tender foliage, and the little plants, and the sorrowful briars. The grass was no longer green, the briars no longer blossomed, the leaves and the plants hung withered and dry about the spot where the virgin had been dishonoured, where the brother had dishonoured his sister.

"Kullervo drew forth his sword, his sharp-edged sword; a long time he looked at it, turning it in his hand, and asking it whether it would feel no pleasure in eating the flesh of the man thus loaded with infamy, in drinking the blood of the man thus covered with crime.

"And the sword knew the heart of the man: it understood the question of the hero. And it made answer to him saying: 'Why indeed should I not

gladly devour the flesh of the man who is loaded
with infamy? Why indeed should I not drink
with pleasure the blood of the man who is bur-
dened with crime? For well I devoured even the
flesh of the innocent man, well can I drink even
the blood of the man who is free from crime.'

"Then Kullervo fixed his sword in the earth,
with the handle downwards and the point upwards, and he threw himself upon the point, and
the point passed through all the depth of his
breast.

"This was the end of all, this was the cruel
destiny of Kullervo, the irrevocable end of the
son of the heroes—the death of the 'Man of Misfortune.' "

You can see how very much unlike other Western poetry this poetry is. The imagination indeed
is of another race and another time than those to
whose literary productions we have become accustomed. But there is beauty here; and the
strangeness of it indicates a possible literary value
by which any literature may be more or less en-
riched. Many are the particular episodes which
rival the beauty and strangeness of the episode of
Kullervo; and I wish that we could have time to
quote them. But I can only refer to them. There
is, for example, the legend of the invention of
music, when the hero Wainamoinen (supposed to
represent the Spirit of the Wind, and the sound
of the name indicates the wailing of the wind) in-

vents the first musical instrument. In no other
literature is there anything quite like this except
in the Greek story of Orpheus. Even as the trees
bent down their heads to listen to the song of
Orpheus, and as the wild beasts became tamed at
the sound, and as the very stones of the road followed to the steps of the musician, so is it in the
"Kalevala." But the Finnish Orpheus is the
greater magician.   To hear him, the sun and moon
come nearer to the earth, the waves of the sea
stop short, bending their heads; the cataracts of
the rivers hang motionless and silent; the fish raise
their heads above the water. And when he plays a
sad melody, all nature weeps with him, even the
trees and the stones and the little plants by the
wayside. And his own tears in falling become
splendid pearls for the crowns of kings.

Then very wonderful too is the story of the
eternal smith, Ilmarinen, who forged the founda-
tions of the world, forged the mountains, forged
the blue sky, so well forging them that nowhere
can be seen the marks of the pincer, the marks of
the hammer, the heads of the nails. Working in
his smithy we see him all grime and black; upon
his head there is one yard deep of iron firing, upon
his shoulders there is one fathom deep of soot—
the soot of the forge; for he seldom has time to
bathe himself. But when the notion takes him
to get married, for the first time he bathes himself, and dresses himself handsomely; then he be-

comes the most beautiful of men. In order to win
his wife he is obliged to perform miracles of
work; yet after he wins her she is killed by wild
beasts. Then he sets to work to forge himself a
wife, a wife of silver, a bride of gold. Very beautiful she is, but she has no heart, and she is always cold, and there is no comfort in her; even
all the magic of the world-maker can not give her
a warm heart. But the work is so beautiful that
he does not like to destroy it. So he takes the
wife of silver, the bride of gold, to the wisest of
heroes, Wainamoinen, and offers her to him as a
gift. But the hero will have no such gift, "Throw
her back into your forged fire, O Ilmarinen," the
hero makes answer—"What greater folly, what
greater sorrow can come upon man than to love
a wife of silver, a bride of gold?"

This pretty story needs no explanation; the
moral is simply "Never marry for money."

Then there is the story of Lemminkainen (this
personality suggested the Pau-puk-keewis of
Longfellow)—the joyous, reckless, handsome,
mischievous pleasure-lover,—always falling into
trouble, because he will not follow his mother's advice, but always loved by her in spite of his follies.
The mother of Lemminkainen is a more wonderful person than the mother of Kullervo. Her son
has been murdered, thrown into a river—the
deepest of all rivers, the river of the dead, the
river of hell. And his mother goes out to find

him. She asks the trees in the forest to tell her where her son is, and she obliges them to answer. But they do not know. She asks the grass, the plants, the animals, the birds; she obliges even the road upon which he walked to talk to her; she talks to the stars and the moon and the sun. Only the sun knows, because he sees everything; and he answers, "Your son is dead, torn to pieces; he has been thrown into the river of Tuoni, the river of hell, the river of the dead." But the mother does not despair. Ilmarinen, the eternal smith, must make for her a rake of brass with teeth long enough to reach into the world of the dead, into the bottom of the abyss; and out of the abyss she brings up the parts of the torn body of her son; she puts them together; she sings over them a magic song; she brings her son to life again, and takes him home. But for a long time he is not able to remember, because he has been dead. After a long time he gets back his memory—only to get into new mischief out of which his mother must help him afresh.

The names of the three heroes quoted to you represent also the names of three great stories, out of the many stories contained in the epics. But in this epic, as in the Indian epics (I mean the Sanskrit epic), there is much more than stories. There are also chapters of moral instruction of a very curious kind—chapters about conduct, the conduct of the parents, the conduct of the chil-

dren, the conduct of the husband, the conduct of
the bride. The instructions to the bride are contained in the twenty-third Rune; there are altogether fifty Runes in the book. This appears to me
likely to interest you, for it is written in relation
to a family system not at all like the family system of the rest of Europe. I think you will find
in it not a little that may remind you of Chinese
teaching on the same subject—the conduct of the
daughter-in-law. But there are of course many
differences, and the most pleasing difference is the
tone of great tenderness in which the instructions
are given. Let us quote some of them:

"O young bride, O my young sister, O my well
beloved and beautiful young flower, listen to the
words which I am going to speak to you, harken
to the lesson which I am going to teach you. You
are going now very far away from us, O beautiful
flower!—you are going to take a long journey, O
my wild-strawberry fruit! you are about to fly
away from us, O most delicate down! you are
about to leave us forever, O velvet tissue—far
away from this habitation you must go, far away
from this beautiful house, to enter another house,
to enter into a strange family. And in that strange
house your position will be very different. There
you will have to walk about with care, to conduct
yourself with prudence, to conduct yourself with
thoughtfulness. There you will not be able, as in
the house of your father, as in the dwelling of

your mother, to run about where you please, to run singing through the valleys, to warble out your songs upon the roadway.

"New habits you must now learn, and forget all the old. You must abandon the love of your father and content yourself with the love of your father-in-law; you must bow very low, you must learn to be generous in the use of courteous words. You must give up old habits and form new ones; you must resign the love of your mother and content yourself with the love of your step-mother: lower must you bow, and you must learn to be lavish in the use of kindly words.

"New habits you must learn and forget the old: you must leave behind you the friendship of your brother, and content yourself with the friendship of your brother-in-law; you must bow lower than you do now; you must learn to be lavish of kindly words.

"New habits you must acquire and forget the old ones; you must leave behind you the friendship of your sister, and be satisfied with the friendship of your sister-in-law; you must learn to make humble reverence, to bow low, to be generous in kindly words.

"If the old man in the corner be to you even like a wolf, if the old woman in her corner be to you even as a she-bear in the house, if the brother-in-law be to you even as a serpent upon the threshold, if the sister-in-law be to you even as a sharp nail,

none the less you must show them each and all
exactly the same respect and the same obedience
that you have been accustomed to display to your
father, to display to your mother, under the roof
of your childhood home."

Then follows a really terrible list of the duties
that she must perform every day from early morning until late at night; to mention them all would
take too long. I quote only a few, enough to
show that the position of a Finnish wife was by
no means an easy one.

"So soon as the cock crows in the morning you
must be quick to rise; you must keep your ears
awake to hear the cry of the cock. And if there
be no cock, or the cock does not crow, then let the
moon be as a cock for you, let the constellation of
the great Bear tell you when it is time to rise.
Then you must quickly make the fire, skilfully
removing the ashes, without sprinkling them upon
the floor. Then quickly go to the stable, clean the
stable, take food to the cattle, feed all the animals
on the farm. For already the cow of your mother-
in-law will be lowing for food; the horse of your
father-in-law will be whinnying; the milch cow of
your sister-in-law will be straining at her tether;
the calf of your brother-in-law will be bleating;
for all will be waiting for her whose duty it is to
give them hay, whose duty it is to give them
food."

Like instructions are given about feeding the

younger animals and the fowls and the little pigs.
But she must not forget the children of the house
at the same time:

"When you have fed the animals and cleaned
the stables come back quickly, quickly as a snow-
storm. For in the chamber the little child has
awakened and has begun to cry in his cradle. He
cannot speak, poor little one; he cannot tell you,
if he be hungry or if he be cold, or if anything
extraordinary has happened to him, before someone that he knows has come to care for him, before he hears the voice of his own mother."

After enumerating and inculcating in the same
manner all the duties of the day, the conduct to
be observed toward every member of the family—
father-in-law, mother-in-law, sister, and brother-
in-law, and the children of them—we find a very
minute code of conduct set forth in regard to
neighbours and acquaintances. The young wife
is especially warned against gossip, against listening to any stories about what happens in other
people's houses, and against telling anybody what
goes on within her own. One piece of advice is
memorable. If the young wife is asked whether
she is well fed, she should reply always that she
has the best of everything which a house can af-
ford, this even if she should have been left without any proper nourishment for several days. Evidently the condition of submission to which Finnish women were reduced by custom was some-

thing much less merciful than has ever been known
in Eastern countries. Only a very generous nature could bear such discipline; and we have many
glimpses in the poem of charming natures of this
kind.

You have seen that merely as a collection of
wonderful stories the Kalevala is of extraordinary
interest, that it is also of interest as describing
the social ethics of a little known people—finally
that it is of interest, of very remarkable interest,
merely as natural poetry—poetry treating of wild
nature, especially rivers and forests and mountains, of the life of the fisher and hunter and wood-
cutter. Indeed, so far as this kind of poetry is
concerned, the "Kalevala" stands alone among the
older productions of European poetry. You do
not find this love of nature in Scandinavian poetry,
nor in Anglo-Saxon poetry, nor in old German
poetry, much less in the earlier form of French,
Italian, or Spanish poetry. The old Northern
poetry comes nearest to it; for in Anglo-Saxon
composition we can find at least wonderful descriptions of the sea, of stones, of the hard life
of sailors. But the dominant tone in Northern
poetry is war; it is in descriptions of battle, or in
accounts of the death of heroes, that the ancient
English or ancient Scandinavian poets excelled. In
Finnish poetry, on the other hand, there is little
or nothing about war. These peaceful people
never had any warlike history; their life was agri-

cultural for the most part, with little or no vio-
lence except such as the excitement of hunting and
fishing could produce. Therefore they had plenty
of time to think about nature, to love nature and
to describe it as no other people of the same
period described it. Striking comparisons have
been made between the Anglo-Saxon Runes, or
charm songs, and Finnish songs of the same kind,
which fully illustrate this difference. Like the
Finns, the early English had magical songs to the
gods of nature—songs for the healing of wounds
and the banishing of sickness. But these are very
commonplace. Not one of them can compare as
poetry with the verses of the Finnish on the same
subject. Here are examples in evidence. The
first is a prayer said when offering food to the
Spirit of the forest, that he might aid the hunter
in his hunting.

"Look, O Kuntar, a fat cake, a cake with
honey, that I may propitiate the forest, that I may
propitiate the forest, that I may entice the thick
forest for the day of my hunting, when I go in
search of prey. Accept my salt, O wood, accept
my porridge, O Tapio, dear king of the wood
with the hat of leaves, with the beard of moss."

And here is a little prayer to the goddess of
water repeated by a sick man taking water as a
medicine.

"O pure water, O Lady of the Water, now do
thou make me whole, lovely as before! for this

I beg thee dearly, and in offering I give thee blood
to appease thee, salt to propitiate thee!"

Or this:

"Goddess of the Sea, mistress of waters, Queen
of a hundred caves, arouse the scaly flocks, urge
on the fishy-crowds forth from their hiding places,
forth from the muddy shrine, forth from the net-
hauling, to the nets of a hundred fishers! Take
now thy beauteous shield, shake the golden water,
with which thou frightenest the fish, and direct
them toward the net beneath the dark level, above
the borders black."

Yet another:

"O vigorous mistress of the wild beasts, sweet
lady of the earth, come with me, be with me,
where I go. Come thou and good luck bring me,
to happy fortune help me. Make thou to move
the foliage, the fruit tree to be shaken, and the
wild beasts drive thither, the largest and the
smallest, with their snouts of every kind, with
their paws of fur of all kinds!"

Now when you look at these little prayers, when
you read them over and observe how pretty they
are, you will also observe that they make little
pictures in the mind. Can not you see the fish glid-
ing over the black border under the dark level of
the water, to the net of a hundred fishers? Can
you not see the "dear king of the wood," with
his hat of leaves and his beard of moss? Can you
not also see in imagination the wild creatures of

the forest with their snouts of many shapes, with
their fur of all kinds? But in Anglo-Saxon poetry
you will not find anything like that. Anglo-Saxon
Rune songs create no images. It is this pictur-
esqueness, this actuality of imagery that is distinctive in Finnish poetry.

In the foregoing part of the lecture I have
chiefly tried to interest you in the "Kalevala."
But aside from interesting you in the book itself as
a story, as a poem, I hope to direct your attention
to a particular feature in Finnish poetry which is
most remote from Japanese poetry. I have
spoken of resemblances as to structure and
method; but it is just in that part of the method
most opposed to Japanese tradition that the greatest interest lies. I do not mean only the use of
natural imagery; I mean much more the use of
parallelism to reinforce that imagery. That is
the thing especially worthy of literary study. Indeed, I think that such study might greatly help
towards a new development, a totally new departure in Japanese verse. In another lecture I spoke
as sincerely as I could of the very high merit in
the epigrammatic forms of Japanese poetry.
These brief forms of poetry have been developed
in Japan to perfection not equalled elsewhere in
modern poetry, perhaps not surpassed, in some
respects, even by Greek poetry of the same kind.
But there can be no doubt of this fact, that a national literature requires many other forms of ex-

pression than the epigrammatic form. Nothing
that is good should ever be despised or cast aside;
but because of its excellences, we should not be
blind to the possibility of other excellences. Now
Japanese literature has other forms of poetry—
forms in which it is possible to produce poems of
immense length, but the spirit of epigrammatic
poetry has really been controlling even these to
a great degree.

I mean that so far as I am able to understand
the subject, the tendency of all Japanese poetry is
to terse expression. Were it not well therefore
to consider at least the possible result of a totally
opposite tendency,—expansion of fancy, luxuri-
ance of expression? Terseness of expression,
pithiness, condensation, are of vast importance in
prose, but poetry has other methods, and the
"Kalevala" is one of the best possible object lessons in the study of such methods, because of the
very simplicity and naturalness with which they are
followed.

Of course there was parallelism in Western
poetry, and all arts of repetition, before anybody
knew anything about the "Kalevala." The most
poetical part of Bible English, as I said, whether
in the Bible itself or in the Book of Common
Prayer, depends almost entirely for its literary
effect upon parallelism, because the old Hebrews,
like the old Finns, practised this art of expression.
Loosely and vaguely it was practised also by many

poets almost unconsciously, who had been particularly influenced by the splendour of the scriptural
translation.   It had figured in prose-poetry as
early as the time of Sir Thomas Browne.   It had
established quite a new idea of poetry even in
America, where the great American poet Poe introduced it into his compositions before Longfellow studied the "Kalevala."   I told you that the
work of Poe, small as it is, had influenced almost
every poet of the great epoch, including Tennyson and the Victorian masters.   But the work even
of Poe was rather instinctive than the result of
any systematic idea.   The systematic idea was
best illustrated when the study of the "Kalevala"
began.

Let us see how Longfellow used the suggestion;
but remember that he was only a beginner, deal-
ing with something entirely new—that he did not
have the strength of Tennyson nor the magical
genius of Swinburne to help him.   He worked
very simply, and probably very rapidly.   There is
a good deal of his song of "Hiawatha" that is
scarcely worthy of praise, and it is difficult to
quote effectively from it, because the charm of the
thing depends chiefly upon its reading as a whole.
Nevertheless there are parts which so well show
or imitate the Finnish spirit, that I must try to
quote them. Take for instance the teaching of
the little Indian child by his grandmother—such

verses as these, where she talks to the little boy
about the milky way in the sky:

> Many things Nokomis taught him
> Of the stars that shine in heaven;
> Showed him Ishkoodah, the comet,
> Ishkoodah, with fiery tresses;
> Showed the Death-Dance of the spirits,
> Warriors with their plumes and war-clubs,
> Flaring far away to northward
> In the frosty nights of Winter;
> Showed the broad, white road in heaven,
> Pathway of the ghosts, the shadows,
> Running straight across the heavens,
> Crowded with the ghosts, the shadows.

Or take again the story of the origin of the
flower commonly called "Dandelion":

> In his life he had one shadow,
> In his heart one sorrow had he.
> Once, as he was gazing northward,
> Far away upon a prairie
> He beheld a maiden standing,
> Saw a tall and slender maiden
> All alone upon a prairie;
> Brightest green were all her garments
> And her hair was like the sunshine.
> Day by day he gazed upon her,
> Day by day he sighed with passion,
> Day by day his heart within him
> Grew more hot with love and longing
> For the maid with yellow tresses.

Observe how the repetition served to represent the growing of the lover's admiration. The same repetition can be used much more effectively in describing weariness and pain, as in the lines about the winter famine:

Oh, the long and dreary Winter!
Oh, the cold and cruel Winter!
Ever thicker, thicker, thicker
Froze the ice on lake and river,
Ever deeper, deeper, deeper
Fell the snow o'er all the landscape,
Fell the covering snow, and drifted
Through the forest, round the village.
Hardly from his buried wigwam
Could the hunter force a passage;
With his mittens and his snow-shoes
Vainly walked he through the forest,
Sought for bird or beast and found none,
Saw no track of deer or rabbit,
In the snow beheld no footprints,
In the ghastly, gleaming forest
Fell, and could not rise from weakness,
Perished there from cold and hunger.
Oh, the famine and the fever!
Oh, the wasting of the famine!
Oh, the blasting of the fever!
Oh, the wailing of the children!
Oh, the anguish of the women!
All the earth was sick and famished;
Hungry was the air around them,
Hungry was the sky above them,

And the hungry stars in heaven
Like the eyes of wolves glared at them!

This is strong, emotionally strong, though it is
not great poetry; but it makes the emotional effect of great poetry by the use of the same means
which the Finnish poets used. The best part of
the poem is the famine chapter, and the next best
is the part entitled "The Ghosts." However, the
charm of a composition can be fully felt only by
those who understand something of the American
Indian's life and the wild northwestern country
described. That is not the immediate matter to
be considered, notwithstanding. The matter to
be considered is whether this method of using parallelism and repetition and alliteration can give
new and great results. I believe that it can, and
that a greater Longfellow would have brought
such results into existence long ago. Of course,
the form is primitive; it does not follow that an
English poet or a Japanese poet should attempt
only a return to primitive methods of poetry in
detail. The detail is of small moment; the spirit
is everything. Parallelism means simply the wish
to present the same idea under a variety of aspects, instead of attempting to put it forward in
one aspect only. Everything great in the way of
thought, everything beautiful in the way of idea,
has many sides. It is merely the superficial
which we can see from the front only; the solid
can be perceived from every possible direction,

and changes shape according to the direction looked at.

The great master of English verse, Swinburne, is also a poet much given to parallelism; for he has found it of incomparable use to him in managing new forms of verse. He uses it in an immense variety of ways—ways impossible to Japanese poets or to Finnish poets; and the splendour of the results can not be imitated in another language. But his case is interesting. The most primitive methods of Finnish poetry, and of ancient poetry in general, coming into his hands, are reproduced into music. I propose to make a few quotations, in illustration. Here are some lines from "Atalanta in Calydon"; they are only parallelisms, but how magnificent they are!

> When thou dravest the men
>   Of the chosen of Thrace,
> None turned him again,
>   Nor endured he thy face
> Close round with the blush of the battle,
>   with light from a terrible place.

Look again at the following lines from "A Song in Time of Revolution":

> There is none of them all that is whole; their lips gape
>   open for breath;
> They are clothed with sickness of soul, and the shape of
>   the shadow of death.

The wind is thwart in their feet; it is full of the shouting
     of mirth;
As one shaketh the sides of a sheet, so it shaketh the ends
     of the earth.

The sword, the sword is made keen; the iron has opened
     its mouth;
The corn is red that was green; 't is bound for the sheaves
     of the south.

The sound of a word was shed, the sound of the wind as
     a breath,
In the ears of the souls that were dead, in the dust of the
     deepness of death.

Where the face of the moon is taken, the ways of the stars
     undone,
The light of the whole sky shaken, the light of the face
     of the sun.

    .   .   .   .   .

Where the sword was covered and hidden, and dust had
     grown in its side,
A word came forth which was bidden, the crying of one
     that cried:

The sides of the two-edged sword shall be bare, and its
     mouth shall be red,
For the breath of the face of the Lord that is felt in the
     bones of the dead.

All this is indeed very grand compared with
anything in the "Kalevala" or in Longfellow's rendering; but do you not see that the grandeur is

also the grandeur of parallelism? Here is proof
of what a master can do with a method older than
Western civilization.   But what is the inference?
Is it not that the old primitive poetry contains
something of eternal value, a value ranging from
the lowest even to the highest, a value that can
lend beauty equally to the song of a little child or
to the thunder of the grandest epic verse?

CHAPTER XIII

THE MOST BEAUTIFUL ROMANCE OF THE MIDDLE AGES

THE value of romantic literature, which has been, so far as the Middle Ages are concerned, unjustly depreciated, does not depend upon beauty of words or beauty of fact. To-day the immense debt of modern literature to the literature of the Middle Ages is better understood; and we are generally beginning to recognize what we owe to the imagination of the Middle Ages, in spite of the ignorance, the superstition and the cruelty of that time. If the evils of the Middle Ages had really been universal, those ages could not have imparted to us lessons of beauty and lessons of nobility having nothing to do with literary form in themselves, yet profoundly affecting modern poetry of the highest class. No; there was very much of moral goodness as well as of moral badness in the Middle Ages; and what was good happened to be very good indeed. Commonly it used to be said (though I do not think any good critic would say it now) that the fervid faith of the time made the moral beauty. Unless we modify this statement a great deal, we can not now accept it at all. There was indeed a religious beauty, particularly mediaeval, but it was not that which created the romance of the period. Indeed, that romantic literature was something of a reaction against the religious restraint upon imagination. But if we mean by mediaeval faith only that which is very much older than any European civilization, and which does not belong to the West any more than to the East—the profound belief in human moral experience—then I think that the statement is true enough. At no time in European history were men more sincere believers in the value of certain virtues than during the Middle Ages—and the very best of the romances are just those romances which illustrate that belief, though not written for a merely ethical purpose.

But I can not better illustrate what I mean than by telling a story, which has nothing to do with Europe, or the Middle Ages, or any particular form of religious belief. It is not a Christian story at all; and it could not be told you exactly as written, for there are some very curious pages in it. But it is a good example of the worth that may lie in a mere product of imagination.

There was a king once, in Persia or Arabia, who, at the time of his accession to power, discovered a wonderful subterranean hall under the garden of his palace. In one chamber of that hall stood six marvellous statues of young girls, each statue being made out of a single diamond. The beauty as well as the cost of the work was beyond imagination. But in the midst of the statues, which stood in a circle, there was an empty pedestal, and on that pedestal was a precious casket containing a letter from the dead father of the king. The letter said:

"O my son, though these statues of girls are indeed beyond all praise, there is yet a seventh statue incomparably more precious and beautiful which I could not obtain before I died. It is now your duty, O my son, to obtain that statue, that it may be placed upon the seventh pedestal. Go, therefore, and ask my favourite slave, who is still alive, how you are to obtain it." Then the young king went in all haste to that old slave, who had been his father's confidant, and showed him the letter. And the old man said, "Even now, O master, I will go with you to find that statue. But it is in one of the three islands in which the genii dwell; and it is necessary, above all things, that you do not fear, and that you obey my instructions in all things. Also, remember that if you make a promise to the Spirits of that land, the promise must be kept."

And they proceeded upon their journey through a great wilderness, in which "nothing existed but grass and the presence of God." I can not try now to tell you about the wonderful things that happened to them, nor about the marvellous boat,

rowed by a boatman having upon his shoulders
the head of an elephant. Suffice it to say that at
last they reached the palace of the king of the
Spirits; and the king came to meet them in the
form of a beautiful old man with a long white
beard. And he said to the young king, "My son,
I will gladly help you, as I helped your father;
and I will give you that seventh statue of diamond
which you desire. But I must ask for a gift in
return. You must bring to me here a young girl,
of about sixteen years old; and she must be very
intelligent; and she must be a true maiden, not only
as to her body, but as to her soul, and heart, and
all her thoughts." The young king thought that
was a very easy thing to find, but the king of the
Spirits assured him that it was not, and further
told him this, "My son, no mortal man is wise
enough to know by his own wisdom the purity that
is in the heart of a young girl. Only by the help
of this magical mirror, which I now lend you, will
you be able to know. Look at the reflection of any
maiden in this mirror, and then, if her heart is
perfectly good and pure, the mirror will remain
bright. But if there be any fault in her, the mirror
will grow dim. Go now, and do my bidding."

You can imagine, of course, what happened
next. Returning to his kingdom, the young king
had brought before him many beautiful girls, the
daughters of the noblest and highest in all the
cities of the land. But in no case did the mirror

remain perfectly clear when the ghostly test was
applied. For three years in vain the king sought;
then in despair he for the first time turned his
attention to the common people. And there came
before him on the very first day a rude man of the
desert, who said, "I know of just such a girl as you
want." Then he went forth and presently returned with a simple girl from the desert, who had
been brought up in the care of her father only,
and had lived with no other companion than the
members of her own family and the camels and
horses of the encampment. And as she stood in
her poor dress before the king, he saw that she
was much more beautiful than any one whom he
had seen before; and he questioned her, only to
find that she was very intelligent; and she was not
at all afraid or ashamed of standing before the
king, but looked about her with large wondering
eyes, like the eyes of a child; and whoever met
that innocent gaze, felt a great joy in his heart,
and could not tell why. And when the king had
the mirror brought, and the reflection of the girl
was thrown upon it, the mirror became much
brighter than before, and shone like a great moon.

There was the maid whom the Spirit-king
wished for. The king easily obtained her from
her parents; but he did not tell her what he intended to do with her. Now it was his duty to
give her to the Spirits; but there was a condition
he found very hard to fulfil. By the terms of his

promise he was not allowed to kiss her, to caress
her, or even to see her, except veiled after the
manner of the country. Only by the mirror had
he been able to know how fair she was. And the
voyage was long; and on the way, the girl, who
thought she was going to be this king's bride,
became sincerely attached to him, after the manner of a child with a brother; and he also in his
heart became much attached to her. But it was
his duty to give her up. At last they reached the
palace of the Spirit-king; and the figure of the old
man came forth and said, "My son, you have done
well and kept your promise. This maiden is all
that I could have wished for; and I accept her.
Now when you go back to your palace, you will
find on the seventh pedestal the statue of the
diamond which your father desired you to obtain."
And, with these words, the Spirit-king vanished,
taking with him the girl, who uttered a great and
piercing cry to heaven at having been thus de-
ceived. Very sorrowfully the young king then
began his journey home. All along the way he
kept regretting that girl, and regretting the cruelty which he had practised in deceiving her and
her parents. And he began to say to himself,
"Accursed be the gift of the king of the Spirits!
Of what worth to me is a woman of diamond any
more than a woman of stone? What is there in
all the world half so beautiful or half so precious

as a living girl such as I discovered? Fool that I was to give her up for the sake of a statue!" But he tried to console himself by remembering that he had obeyed his dead father's wish.

Still, he could not console himself. Reaching his palace, he went to his secret chamber to weep alone, and he wept night and day, in spite of the efforts of his ministers to comfort him. But at last one of them said, "O my king, in the hall beneath your garden there has appeared a wonderful statue upon the seventh pedestal; perchance if you go to see it, your heart will become more joyful."

Then with great reluctance the king properly dressed himself, and went to the subterranean hall.

There indeed was the statue, the gift of the Spirit-king; and very beautiful it was. But it was not made of diamond, and it looked so strangely like the girl whom he had lost, that the king's heart leapt in his breast for astonishment. He put out his hand and touched the statue, and found it warm with life and youth. And a sweet voice said to him, "Yes, it is really I—have you forgotten?"

Thus she was given back to him; and the Spirit-king came to their wedding, and thus addressed the bridegroom, "O my son, for your dead father's sake I did this thing. For it was meant to

teach you that the worth of a really pure and perfect woman is more than the price of any diamond
or any treasure that the earth can yield."

Now you can see at once the beauty of this
story; and the moral of it is exactly the same as
that of the famous verse, in the Book of Proverbs, "Who can find a virtuous woman? for her
price is far above rubies." But it is simply a story
from the "Arabian Nights"—one of those stories
which you will not find in the ordinary European
translations, because it is written in such a way
that no English translator except Burton would
have dared to translate it quite literally. The ob-
scenity of parts of the original does not really
detract in the least from the beauty and tenderness of the motive of the story; and we must remember that what we call moral or immoral in
style depends very much upon the fashion of an
age and time.

Now it is exactly the same kind of moral charm
that distinguishes the best of the old English romances—a charm which has nothing to do with
the style, but everything to do with the feeling
and suggestion of the composition. But in some
of the old romances, the style too has a very great
charm of quaintness and simplicity and sincerity
not to be imitated to-day. In this respect the older
French romances, from which the English made
their renderings, are much the best. And the best
of all is said to be "Amis and Amile," which the

English rendered as "Amicus and Amelius."
Something of the story ought to interest you.

The whole subject of this romance is the virtue
of friendship, though this of course involves a
number of other virtues quite as distinguished.
Amis and Amile, that is to say Amicus and Amelius, are two young knights who at the beginning
of their career become profoundly attached to
each other. Not content with the duties of this
natural affection, they imposed upon themselves
all the duties which chivalry also attached to the
office of friend. The romance tells of how they
triumphed over every conceivable test to which
their friendship was subjected. Often and often
the witchcraft of woman worked to separate them,
but could not. Both married, yet after marriage
their friendship was just as strong as before.
Each has to fight many times on account of the
other, and suffer all things which it is most hard
for a proud and brave man to bear. But everything is suffered cheerfully, and the friends are
such true knights that, in all their trials, neither
does anything wrong, or commits the slightest
fault against truth—until a certain sad day. On
that day it is the duty of Amis to fight in a trial
by battle. But he is sick, and can not fight; then
to save his honour his friend Amile puts on the
armour and helmet of Amis, and so pretending to
be Amis, goes to the meeting place, and wins the
fight gloriously. But this was an act of untruthful-

ness; he had gone into battle under a false name, and to do anything false even for a good motive is bad. So heaven punishes him by afflicting him with the horrible disease of leprosy.

The conditions of leprosy in the Middle Ages were of a peculiar kind. The disease seems to have been introduced into Europe from Asia— perhaps by the Crusaders. Michelet suggests that it may have resulted from the European want of cleanliness, brought about by ascetic teachings— for the old Greek and Roman public bath-houses were held in horror by the mediæval Church. But this is not at all certain. What is certain is that in the thirteenth, fourteenth and fifteenth centuries leprosy became very prevalent. The disease was not then at all understood; it was supposed to be extremely contagious, and the man afflicted by it was immediately separated from society, and not allowed to live in any community under such conditions as could bring him into contact with other inhabitants. His wife or children could accompany him only on the terrible condition of being considered lepers. Every leper wore a kind of monk's dress, with a hood covering the face; and he had to carry a bell and ring it constantly to give notice of his approach. Special leper-houses were built near every town, where such unfortunates might obtain accommodation. They were allowed to beg, but it was considered dangerous to go very near them, so that in most cases

alms or food would be thrown to them only, instead of being put into their hands.

Now when the victim of leprosy in this romance
is first afflicted by the disease, he happens to be
far away from his good friend. And none of his
own family is willing to help him; he is regarded
with superstitious as well as with physical horror.
There is nothing left for him to do but to yield
up his knighthood and his welfare and his family,
to put on the leper's robe, and to go begging along
the roads, carrying a leper's bell. And this he
does. For long, long months he goes begging
·from town to town, till at last, by mere chance,
he finds his way to the gate of the great castle
where his good friend is living—now a great
prince, and married to the daughter of the king.
And he asks at the castle gate for charity and for
food.

Now the porter at the gate observes that the
leper has a very beautiful cup, exactly resembling
a drinking cup belonging to his master, and he
thinks it his duty to tell these things to the lord
of the castle. And the lord of the castle remembers that very long ago he and his friend each
had a cup of this kind, given to them by the bishop
of Rome. So, hearing the porter's story, he knew
that the leper at the gate was the friend who "had
delivered him from death, and won for him the
daughter of the King of France to be his wife."
Here I had better quote from the French version

of the story, in which the names of the friends
are changed, but without changing the beauty of
the tale itself:

"And straightway he fell upon him, and began
to weep greatly, and kissed him. And when his
wife heard that, she ran out with her hair in dis-
array, weeping and distressed exceedingly—for
she remembered that it was he who had slain the
false Ardres. And thereupon they placed him in
a fair bed, and said to him, 'Abide with us until
God's will be accomplished in thee, for all that
we have is at thy service.' So he abode with
them."

You must understand, by the allusion to "God's
will," that leprosy was in the Middle Ages really
considered to be a punishment from heaven—so
that in taking a leper into his castle, the good
friend was not only offending against the law of
the land, but risking celestial punishment as well,
according to the notions of that age. His charity,
therefore, was true charity indeed, and his friendship without fear. But it was going to be put to
a test more terrible than any ever endured before.
To comprehend what followed, you must know
that there was one horrible superstition of the
Middle Ages—the belief that by bathing in human
blood the disease of leprosy might be cured.
Murders were often committed under the influence
of that superstition. I believe you will remember
that the "Golden Legend" of Longfellow is

founded upon a mediaeval story in which a young
girl voluntarily offers up her life in order that
her blood may cure the leprosy of her king.   In
the present romance there is much more tragedy.
One night while sleeping in his friend's castle, the
leper was awakened by an angel from God—
Raphael—who said to him:

"I am Raphael, the angel of the Lord, and
I am come to tell thee how thou mayst be healed.
Thou shalt bid Amile thy comrade that he slay
his two children and wash thee in their blood, and
so thy body shall be made whole."   And Amis
said to him, "Let not this thing be, that my comrade should become a murderer for my sake."
But the angel said, "It is convenient that he do
this."   And thereupon the angel departed.

The phrase, "it is convenient," must be understood as meaning, "it is ordered."   For the mediaeval lord used such gentle expressions when
issuing his commands; and the angel talked like
a feudal messenger.   But in spite of the command,
the sick man does not tell his friend about the
angel's visit, until Amile, who has overheard
the voice, forces him to acknowledge whom he had
been talking with during the night.   And the emotion of the lord may be imagined, though he
utters it only in the following gentle words—"I
would have given to thee my man servants and
my maid servants and all my goods—and thou
feignest that an angel hath spoken to thee that I

should slay my two children. But I conjure thee
by the faith which there is between me and thee,
and by our comradeship, and by the baptism we
received together, that thou tell me whether it
was man or angel said that to thee."

Amis declares that it was really an angel, and
Amile never thinks of doubting his friend's
word. It would be a pity to tell you the sequel in
my own words; let me quote again from the text,
translated by Walter Pater. I think you will find
it beautiful and touching:

"Then Amile began to weep in secret, and
thought within himself, 'If this man was ready
to die before the King for me, shall I not for him
slay my children? Shall I not keep faith with
him who was faithful to me even unto death?'
And Amile tarried no longer, but departed to
the chamber of his wife, and bade her go to hear
the Sacred Office. And he took a sword, and
went to the bed where the children were lying,
and found them asleep. And he lay down over
them and began to weep bitterly and said, 'Has
any man yet heard of a father who of his own
will slew his children? Alas, my children! I am
no longer your father, but your cruel murderer.'

"And the children awoke at the tears of their
father, which fell upon them; and they looked up
into his face and began to laugh. And as they
were of age about three years, he said, 'Your
laughing will be turned into tears, for your inno-

cent blood must now be shed'; and therewith he
cut off their heads. Then he laid them back in
the bed, and put the heads upon the bodies, and
covered them as though they slept; and with the
blood which he had taken he washed his comrade,
and said, 'Lord Jesus Christ! who hast com-
manded men to keep faith on earth, and didst heal
the leper by Thy word! cleanse now my comrade,
for whose love I have shed the blood of my children.'" And of course the leper is immediately
and completely cured. But the mother did not
know anything about the killing of the children;
we have to hear something about her share in the
tragedy. Let me again quote, this time giving the
real and very beautiful conclusion—

"Now neither the father nor the mother had
yet entered where the children were, but the father
sighed heavily because they were dead, and the
mother asked for them, that they might rejoice
together; but Amile said, 'Dame! let the children
sleep.' And it was already the hour of Tierce.
And going in alone to the children to weep over
them, he found them at play in the bed; only, in
the place of the sword-cuts about their throats
was, as it were, a thread of crimson. And he
took them in his arms and carried them to his wife
and said, 'Rejoice greatly! For thy children whom
I had slain by the commandment of the angel,
are alive, and by their blood is Amis healed.'"

I think you will all see how fine a story this is,

and feel the emotional force of the grand moral idea behind it. There is nothing more to tell you, except the curious fact that during the Middle Ages, when it was believed that the story was really true, Amis and Amile—or Amicus and Amelius— were actually considered by the Church as saints, and people used to pray to them. When anybody was anxious for his friend, or feared that he might lose the love of his friend, or was afraid that he might not have strength to perform his duty as friend—then he would go to church to implore help from the good saints Amicus and Amelius. But of course it was all a mistake—a mistake which lasted until the end of the seventeenth century! Then somebody called the attention of the Church to the unmistakable fact that Amicus and Amelius were merely inventions of some mediae- val romancer. Then the Church made investi- gation, and greatly shocked, withdrew from the list of its saints those long-loved names of Amicus and Amelius—a reform in which I cannot help thinking the Church made a very serious mistake. What matter whether those shadowy figures rep- resented original human lives or only human dreams? They were beautiful, and belief in them made men think beautiful thoughts, and the im- agined help from them had comforted many thousands of hearts. It would have been better to have left them alone; for that matter, how many of the existent lives of saints are really true?

Nevertheless the friends are not dead, though ex-
pelled from the heaven of the Church. They still
live in romance; and everybody who reads about
them feels a little better for their acquaintance.

What I read to you was from the French version—that is much the more beautiful of the two.
You will find some extracts from the English version in the pages of Ten Brink. But as that great
German scholar pointed out, the English story
is much rougher than the French. For example,
in the English story, the knight rushes out of his
castle to beat the leper at the gate, and to accuse
him of having stolen the cup. And he does beat
him ferociously, and abuses him with very vio-
lent terms. In fact, the English writer reflected
too much of mediaeval English character, in trying to cover, or to improve upon, the French
story, which was the first. In the French
story all is knightly smooth, refined as well as
simple and strong. And where did the mediaeval
imagination get its material for the story? Partly,
perhaps, from the story of Joseph in the Bible,
partly from the story of Abraham; but the scriptural material is so admirably worked over that
the whole thing appears deliciously original. That
was the great art of the Middle Ages—to make
old, old things quite new by the magic of spiritual
imagination. Men then lived in a world of
dreams. And that world still attracts us, for the
simple reason that happiness chiefly consists in

dreams.   Exact science may help us a great deal, no doubt, but mathematics do not make us any happier.   Dreams do, if we can believe them. The Middle Ages could believe them; we, at the best, can only try.

CHAPTER XIV

"IONICA"

I AM going now to talk about a very rare kind of poetry in a very rare little book, like fine wine in a small and precious flask. The author never put his name to the book—indeed for many years it was not known who wrote the volume. We now know that the author was a school teacher called William Johnson who, later in life, coming into a small fortune, changed his name to William Cory. He was born sometime about 1823, and died in 1892. He was, I believe, an Oxford man and was assistant master of Eton College for a number of years. Judging from his poems, he must have found pleasure in his profession as well as pain. There is a strange sadness nearly always, but this sadness is mixed with expressions of love for the educational establishment which he directed, and for the students whose minds he helped to form. He must have been otherwise a very shy man. Scarcely anything seems to be known about him after his departure from educational circles, although everybody of taste now knows his poems. I wish to speak of them because I think that literary graduates of this uni-

versity ought to be at least familiar with the name
"Ionica." At all events you should know something about the man and about the best of his
poems. If you should ask why so little has yet
been said about him in books on English literature,
I would answer that in the first place he was a
very small poet writing in the time of giants,
having for competitors Tennyson, Browning and
others. He could scarcely make his small pipe
heard in the thunder of those great organ tones.
In the second place his verses were never written
to please the public at all. They were written
only for fine scholars, and even the titles of many
of them cannot be explained by a person devoid
of some Greek culture. So the little book, which
appeared quite early in the Victorian Age, was
soon forgotten. Being forgotten it ran out of
print and disappeared. Then somebody remembered that it had existed. I have told you that
it was like the tone of a little pipe or flute as
compared with the organ music of the larger
poets. But the little pipe happened to be a Greek
pipe—the melody was very sweet and very
strange and old, and people who had heard it
once soon wanted to hear it again. But they could
not get it. Copies of the first edition fetched extraordinary sums. Some few years ago a new
edition appeared, but this too is now out of print
and is fetching fancy prices. However, you must
not expect anything too wonderful from this way

of introducing the subject. The facts only show
that the poems are liked by persons of refinement
and wealth. I hope to make you like some of
them, but the difficulties of so doing are considerable, because of the extremely English character
of some pieces and the extremely Greek tone of
others. There is also some uneven work. The
poet is not in all cases successful. Sometimes he
tried to write society verse, and his society verse
must be considered a failure. The best pieces are
his Greek pieces and some compositions on love
subjects of a most delicate and bewitching kind.

Of course the very name "Ionica" suggests
Greek work, a collection of pieces in Ionic style.
But you must not think that this means only repetitions of ancient subjects. This author brings the
Greek feeling back again into the very heart of
English life sometimes, or makes an English fact
illustrate a Greek fable. Some delightful translations from the Greek there are, but less than half
a dozen in all.

I scarcely know how to begin—what piece to
quote first. But perhaps the little fancy called
"Mimnermus in Church" is the best known, and
the one which will best serve to introduce us to
the character of Cory. Before quoting it, however, I must explain the title briefly. Mimnermus
was an old Greek philosopher and poet who
thought that all things in the world are temporary, that all hope of a future life is vain, that

there is nothing worth existing for except love, and that without affection one were better dead. There are, no doubt, various modern thinkers who tell you much the same thing, and this little poem exhibits such modern feeling in a Greek dress. I mean that we have here a picture of a young man, a young English scholar, listening in church to Christian teaching, but answering that teaching with the thought of the old Greeks. There is of course one slight difference; the modern conception of love is perhaps a little wider in range than that of the old Greeks. There is more of the ideal in it.

MIMNERMUS IN CHURCH

You promise heavens free from strife,
    Pure truth, and perfect change of will;
But sweet, sweet is this human life,
    So sweet, I fain would breathe it still;
Your chilly stars I can forego,
This warm kind world is all I know.

You say there is no substance here,
    One great reality above:
Back from that void I shrink in fear
    And child-like hide myself in love;
Show me what angels feel. Till then
I cling, a mere weak man, to men.

You bid me lift my mean desires
    From faltering lips and fitful veins

To sexless souls, ideal choirs,
   Unwearied voices, wordless strains;
My mind with fonder welcome owns
One dear dead friend's remembered tones.

Forsooth the present we must give
   To that which cannot pass away;
All beauteous things for which we live
   By laws of time and space decay.
But oh, the very reason why
I clasp them, is because they die.

The preacher has been talking to his congregation about the joys of Heaven. There, he says, there will be no quarrelling, no contest, no falsehood, and all evil dispositions will be entirely changed to good. The poet answers, "This world and this life are full of beauty and of joy for me. I do not want to die, I want to live. I do not wish to go to that cold region of stars about which you teach. I only know this world and I find in it warm hearts and precious affection. You say that this world is a phantom, unsubstantial, unreal, and that the only reality is above, in Heaven. To me that Heaven appears but as an awful emptiness. I shrink from it in terror, and like a child seek for consolation in human love. It is no use to talk to me about angels until you can prove to me that angels can feel happier than men. I prefer to remain with human beings. You say that I ought to wish for higher things than this world can give, that here minds are unsteady and weak,

hearts fickle and selfish, and you talk of souls without sex, imaginary concerts of perfect music, tire-
less singing in Heaven, and the pleasure of conversation without speech.   But all the happiness
that we know is received from our fellow beings.
I remember the voice of one dead friend with
deeper love and pleasure than any images of
Heaven could ever excite in my mind."

The last stanza needs no paraphrasing, but it
deserves some comment, for it is the expression of
one great difference between the old Greek feeling
in regard to life and death, and all modern religious feeling on the same subject.   You can read
through hundreds of beautiful inscriptions which
were placed over the Greek tombs.   They are contained in the Greek Anthology.   You will find
there almost nothing about hope of a future life,
or about Heaven.   They are not for the most part
sad; they are actually joyous in many cases.   You
would say that the Greek mind thought thus about
death—"I have had my share of the beauty and
the love of this world, and I am grateful for this
enjoyment, and now it is time to go to sleep."
There is actually an inscription to the effect, "I
have supped well of the banquet of life."   The
Eastern religions, including Christianity, taught
that because everything in the world is uncertain,
impermanent, perishable, therefore we ought not
to allow our minds to love worldly things.   But
the Greek mind, as expressed by the old epigraphy

in the cemeteries, not less than by the teaching
of Mimnermus, took exactly the opposite view.
"O children of men, it is because beauty and pleasure and love and light can last only for a little
while, it is exactly because of this that you should
love them. Why refuse to enjoy the present because it can not last for ever?" And at a much
later day the Persian poet Omar took, you will
remember, precisely the same view. You need
not think that it would be wise to accept such
teaching for a rule of life, but it has a certain
value as a balance to the other extreme view, that
we should make ourselves miserable in this world
with the idea of being rewarded in another, concerning which we have no positive knowledge.
The lines with which the poem concludes at least
deserve to be thought about—

> But oh, the very reason why
> I clasp them, is because they die.

We shall later on take some of the purely Greek
work of Cory for study, but I want now to interest you in the more modern part of it. The
charm of the following passage you will better
feel by remembering that the writer was then a
schoolmaster at Eton, and that the verses particularly express the love which he felt for his students—a love the more profound, perhaps, because the circumstances of the teacher's position
obliged him to appear cold and severe, obliged

him to suppress natural impulses of affection and generosity. The discipline of the masters in English public schools is much more severe than the discipline to which the students are subjected. The boys enjoy a great deal of liberty. The masters may be said to have none. Yet there are men so constituted that they learn to greatly love the profession. The title of this poem is "Reparabo," which means "I will atone."

> The world will rob me of my friends,
>   For time with her conspires;
> But they shall both, to make amends,
>   Relight my slumbering fires.
>
> For while my comrades pass away
>   To bow and smirk and gloze,
> Come others, for as short a stay;
>   And dear are these as those.
>
> And who was this? they ask; and then
>   The loved and lost I praise:
> " Like you they frolicked; they are men;
>   Bless ye my later days."
>
> Why fret? The hawks I trained are flown;
>   'Twas nature bade them range;
> I could not keep their wings half-grown,
>   I could not bar the change.
>
> With lattice opened wide I stand
>   To watch their eager flight;
> With broken jesses in my hand
>   I muse on their delight.

And oh! if one with sullied plume
   Should droop in mid career,
My love makes signals,—" There is room,
   O bleeding wanderer, here."

This comparison of the educator to a falconer, and of the students to young hawks eager to break their jesses, seems to an Englishman particularly happy in reference to Eton, from which so many youths pass into the ranks of the army and navy. The line about bowing, smirking and glozing, refers to the comparative insincerity of the higher society into which so many of the scholars must eventually pass. "Smirking" suggests insincere smiles, "glozing" implies tolerating or lightly passing over faults or wrongs or serious matters that should not be considered lightly. Society is essentially insincere and artificial in all countries, but especially so in England. The old Eton master thinks, however, that he knows the moral character of the boys, the strong principles which make its foundation, and he trusts that they will be able in a general way to do only what is right, in spite of conventions and humbug.

As I told you before, we know very little about the personal life of Cory, who must have been a very reserved man; but a poet puts his heart into his verses as a general rule, and there are many little poems in this book that suggest to us an unhappy love episode. These are extremely pretty and touching, the writer in most cases confessing himself unworthy of the person who charmed him; but the finest thing of the kind is a composition which he suggestively entitled "A Fable"—that is to say, a fable in the Greek sense, an emblem or symbol of truth.

> An eager girl, whose father buys
>   Some ruined thane's forsaken hall,
> Explores the new domain and tries
>   Before the rest to view it all.

I think you have often noted the fact here related; when a family moves to a new house, it is the child, or the youngest daughter, who is the first to explore all the secrets of the new residence, and whose young eyes discover things which the older folks had not noticed.

> Alone she lifts the latch, and glides,
>   Through many a sadly curtained room,
> As daylight through the doorway slides
>   And struggles with the muffled gloom.

> With mimicries of dance she wakes
>   The lordly gallery's silent floor,
> And climbing up on tiptoe, makes
>   The old-world mirror smile once more.

> With tankards dry she chills her lips,
>   With yellowing laces veils the head,
> And leaps in pride of ownership
>   Upon the faded marriage bed.

A harp in some dark nook she sees
  Long left a prey to heat and frost,
She smites it; can such tinklings please?
  Is not all worth, all beauty, lost?

Ah, who'd have thought such sweetness clung
  To loose neglected strings like those?
They answered to whate'er was sung,
  And sounded as a lady chose.

Her pitying finger hurried by
  Each vacant space, each slackened chord;
Nor would her wayward zeal let die
  The music-spirit she restored.

The fashion quaint, the timeworn flaws,
  The narrow range, the doubtful tone,
All was excused awhile, because
  It seemed a creature of her own.

Perfection tires; the new in old,
  The mended wrecks that need her skill,
Amuse her. If the truth be told,
  She loves the triumph of her will.

With this, she dares herself persuade,
  She'll be for many a month content,
Quite sure no duchess ever played
  Upon a sweeter instrument.

And thus in sooth she can beguile
  Girlhood's romantic hours, but soon
She yields to taste and mood and style,
  A siren of the gay saloon.

And wonders how she once could like
　　Those drooping wires, those failing notes,
And leaves her toy for bats to strike
　　Amongst the cobwebs and the motes.

But enter in, thou freezing wind,
　　And snap the harp-strings, one by one;
It was a maiden blithe and kind:
　　They felt her touch; their task is done.

In this charming little study we know that the
harp described is not a harp; it is the loving heart
of an old man, at least of a man beyond the usual
age of lovers. He has described and perhaps
adored some beautiful person who seemed to care
for him, and who played upon his heart, with her
whims, caresses, smiles, much as one would play
upon the strings of a harp. She did not mean to
be cruel at all, nor even insincere. It is even
probable that she really in those times thought
that she loved the man, and under the charms of
the girl the man became a different being; the old-
fashioned mind brightened, the old-fashioned
heart exposed its hidden treasures of tenderness
and wisdom and sympathy. Very much like playing upon a long forgotten instrument, was the relation between the maiden and the man—not only
because he resembled such an instrument in the
fact of belonging emotionally and intellectually to
another generation, but also because his was a

heart whose true music had long been silent, un-
heard by the world. Undoubtedly the maiden
meant no harm, but she caused a great deal of
pain, for at a later day, becoming a great lady
of society, she forgot all about this old friendship,
or perhaps wondered why she ever wasted her
time in talking to such a strange old-fashioned
professor. Then the affectionate heart is condemned to silence again, to silence and oblivion,
like the harp thrown away in some garret to be
covered with cobwebs and visited only by bats.
"Is it not time," the old man thinks, "that the
strings should be broken, the strings of the heart?
Let the cold wind of death now come and snap
them." Yet, after all, why should he complain?
Did he not have the beautiful experience of loving, and was she not in that time at least well
worthy of the love that she called forth like
music?

There are several other poems referring to
what would seem to be the same experience, and
all are beautiful, but one seems to me nobler than
the rest, expressing as it does a generous resigna-
tion. It is called "Deteriora," a Latin word signifying lesser, inferior, or deteriorated things—
not easy to translate. Nor would you find the
poem easy to understand, referring as it does to
conditions of society foreign to anything in Japanese experience. But some verses which I may
quote you will like.

If fate and nature screen from me
  The sovran front I bowed before,
And set the glorious creature free,
  Whom I would clasp, detain, adore,—
If I forego that strange delight,
Must all be lost? Not quite, not quite.

Die, Little Love, without complaint,
  Whom honour standeth by to shrive:
Assoilèd from all selfish taint,
  Die, Love, whom Friendship will survive.
Not hate nor folly gave thee birth;
And briefness does but raise thy worth.

This is the same thought which Tennyson expressed in his famous lines,

  'Tis better to have loved and lost
  Than never to have loved at all.

But it is still more finely expressed to meet a particular personal mood. One must not think the world lost because a woman has been lost, he says, and such a love is not a thing for any man to be ashamed of, in spite of the fact that it has been disappointed. It was honourable, unselfish, not inspired by any passion or any folly, and the very brevity of the experience only serves to make it more precious. Observe the use of the words "shrive" and "assoiled." These refer to the old religious custom of confession; to "shrive" signifies to forgive, to free from sin, as a priest is supposed to do, and "assoiled" means "purified."

If this was a personal experience, it must have
been an experience of advanced life. Elsewhere
the story of a boyish love is told very prettily,
under the title of "Two Fragments of Childhood." This is the first fragment:

> When these locks were yellow as gold,
> When past days were easily told,
> Well I knew the voice of the sea,
> Once he spake as a friend to me.
> Thunder-rollings carelessly heard,
> Once that poor little heart they stirred,
>> Why, Oh, why?
>> Memory, memory!
> She that I wished to be with was by.
>
> Sick was I in those misanthrope days
> Of soft caresses, womanly ways;
> Once that maid on the stair I met
> Lip on brow she suddenly set.
> Then flushed up my chivalrous blood,
> Like Swiss streams in a mid-summer flood.
>> Then, Oh, then,
>> Imogen, Imogen!
> Hadst thou a lover, whose years were ten.

This is evidently the charming memory of a
little sick boy sent to the seaside for his health,
according to the English custom, and unhappy
there, unable to play about like stronger children,
and obliged to remain under the constant care of
nurses and female relatives. But in the same
house there is another family with a beautiful

young daughter, probably sixteen or eighteen
years old. The little boy wishes, wishes so much
that the beautiful lady would speak to him and
play with him, but he is shy, afraid to approach
her—only looks at her with great admiring loving
eyes. But one day she meets him on the stairs,
and stoops down and kisses him on the forehead.
Then he is in Heaven. Afterward no doubt she
played with him, and they walked up and down
by the shore of the sea together, and now, though
an old man, whenever he hears the roar of the
sea he remembers the beautiful lady who played
with him and caressed him, when he was a little
sick child. How much he loved her! But she
was a woman, and he was only ten years old. The
reference to "chivalrous blood" signifies just this,
that at the moment when she kissed him he would
have given his life for her, would have dared anything or done anything to show his devotion to
her. No prettier memory of a child could be told.

We can learn a good deal about even the shyest
of the poets through a close understanding of his
poetry. From the foregoing we know that Cory
must have been a sickly child; and from other
poems referring to school life we can not escape
the supposition that he was not a strong lad. In
one of his verses he speaks of being unable to join
in the hearty play of his comrades; and in the
poem which touches on the life of the mature man
we find him acknowledging that he believed his

life a failure—a failure through want of strength.
I am going to quote this poem for other reasons.
It is a beautiful address either to some favourite
student or to a beloved son—it is impossible to
decide which. But that does not matter. The
title is "A New Year's Day."

Our planet runs through liquid space,
And sweeps us with her in the race;
And wrinkles gather on my face,
    And Hebe bloom on thine:
Our sun with his encircling spheres
Around the central sun careers;
And unto thee with mustering years
    Come hopes which I resign.

'Twere sweet for me to keep thee still
Reclining halfway up the hill;
But time will not obey the will,
    And onward thou must climb:
'Twere sweet to pause on this descent,
To wait for thee and pitch my tent,
But march I must with shoulders bent,
    Yet further from my prime.

I shall not tread thy battlefield,
Nor see the blazon on thy shield;
Take thou the sword I could not wield,
    And leave me, and forget.
Be fairer, braver, more admired;
So win what feeble hearts desired;
Then leave thine arms, when thou art tired,
    To some one nobler yet.

How beautiful this is, and how profoundly sad!

I shall return to the personal poetry of Cory later on, but I want now to give you some examples of his Greek work. Perhaps the best of this is little more than a rendering of Greek into English; some of the work is pure translation. But it is the translation of a very great master, the perfect rendering of Greek feeling as well as of Greek thought. Here is an example of pure translation:

They told me, Heraclitus, they told me you were dead,
They brought me bitter news to hear and bitter tears to
　　shed.
I wept, as I remembered, how often you and I
Had tired the sun with talking and sent him down the
　　sky.
And now that thou art lying, my dear old Carian guest,
A handful of grey ashes, long, long ago at rest,
Still are thy pleasant voices, thy nightingales, awake;
For Death, he taketh all away, but them he cannot take.

What are "thy pleasant voices, thy nightingales"? They are the songs which the dear dead poet made, still sung in his native country, though his body was burned to ashes long ago—has been changed into a mere handful of grey ashes, which, doubtless, have been placed in an urn, as is done with such ashes to-day in Japan. Death takes away all things from man, but not his poems, his songs, the beautiful thoughts which he puts into musical verse. These will always be heard like nightingales. The fourth line in the first stanza contains an idiom which may not be familiar to you. It means only that the two friends talked all day until the sun set in the West, and still talked on after that. Tennyson has used the same Greek thought in a verse of his poem, "A Dream of Fair Women," where Cleopatra says,

> "We drank the Libyan sun to sleep."

The Greek author of the above poem was the great poet Callimachus, and the English translator does not think it necessary even to give the name, as he wrote only for folk well acquainted with the classics. He has another short translation which he accompanies with the original Greek text; it is very pretty, but of an entirely different kind, a kind that may remind you of some Japanese poems. It is only about a cicada and a peasant girl, and perhaps it is twenty-four or twenty-five hundred years old.

> A dry cicale chirps to a lass making hay,
> "Why creak'st thou, Tithonus?" quoth she. "I don't play;
> It doubles my toil, your importunate lay,
> I've earned a sweet pillow, lo! Hesper is nigh;
> I clasp a good wisp and in fragrance I lie;
> But thou art unwearied, and empty, and dry."

How very human this little thing is—how actually it brings before us the figure of the girl, who must

have become dust some time between two and
three thousand years ago! She is working hard
in the field, and the constant singing of the insect
prompts her to make a comical protest. "Oh,
Tithonus, what are you making that creaking
noise for? You old dry thing, I have no time to
play with you, or to idle in any way, but you do
nothing but complain. Why don't you work, as I
do? Soon I shall have leave to sleep, because
I have worked well. There is the evening star,
and I shall have a good bed of hay, sweet-smelling
fresh hay, to lie upon. How well I shall sleep.
But you, you idle noisy thing, you do not deserve
to sleep. You have done nothing to tire you.
And you are empty, dry and thirsty. Serves you
right!" Of course you recognize the allusion to
the story of Tithonus, so beautifully told by Tennyson. The girl's jest has a double meaning.
The word "importunate" has the signification of
a wearisome repetition of a request, a constant
asking, impossible to satisfy. Tithonus was supposed to complain because he was obliged to live
although he wanted to die. That young girl does
not want to die at all. And she says that the noise
of the insect, supposed to repeat the complaint of
Tithonus, only makes it more tiresome for her to
work. She was feeling, no doubt, much as a Japanese student would feel when troubled by the
singing of *semi* on some very hot afternoon while
he is trying to master some difficult problem.

That is pure Greek—pure as another mingling
of the Greek feeling with the modern scholarly
spirit, entitled "An Invocation." Before quoting
from it I must explain somewhat; otherwise you
might not be able to imagine what it means, because it was written to be read by those only who
are acquainted with Theocritus and the Greek
idylists. Perhaps I had better say something too,
about the word idyl, for the use of the word by
Tennyson is not the Greek use at all, except in
the mere fact that the word signifies a picturing,
a shadowing or an imagining of things. Tennyson's pictures are of a purely imaginative kind in
the "Idyls of the King." But the Greek poets
who first invented the poetry called idyllic did not
attempt the heroic works of imagination at all;
they only endeavoured to make perfectly true pictures of the common life of peasants in the country. They wrote about the young men and young
girls working on the farms, about the way they
quarrelled or rejoiced or made love, about their
dances and their songs, about their religious fes-
tivals and their sacrifices to the gods at the parish
temple. Imagine a Japanese scholar of to-day
who, after leaving the university, instead of busy-
ing himself with the fashionable studies of the
time, should go out into the remoter districts or
islands of Japan, and devote his life to studying
the existence of the commoner people there, and
making poems about it. This was exactly what

the Greek idylists did,—that is, the best of them. They were great scholars and became friends of kings, but they wrote poetry chiefly about peasant life, and they gave all their genius to the work. The result was so beautiful that everybody is still charmed by the pictures or idyls which they made.

Well, after this disgression, to return to the subject of Theocritus, the greatest of the idylists. He has often introduced into his idyls the name of Comatas. Who was Comatas? Comatas was a Greek shepherd boy, or more strictly speaking a goatherd, who kept the flocks of a rich man. It was his duty to sacrifice to the gods none of his master's animals, without permission; but as his master was a very avaricious person, Comatas knew that it would be of little use to ask him. Now this Comatas was a very good singer of peasant songs, and he made many beautiful poems for the people to sing, and he believed that it was the gods who had given him power to make the songs, and the Muses had inspired him with the capacity to make good verse. In spite of his master's will, Comatas therefore thought it was not very bad to take the young kids and sacrifice to the gods and the Muses. When his master found out what had been done with the animals, naturally he became very angry, and he put Comatas into a great box of cedar-wood in order to starve him to death—saying, as he closed and locked the lid, "Now, Comatas, let us see whether the gods

will feed you!" In that box Comatas was left
for a year without food or drink, and when the
master, at the end of the year, opened the box,
he expected to find nothing but the bones of the
goatherd. But Comatas was alive and well, singing sweet songs, because during the year the Muses
had sent bees to feed him with honey. The bees
had been able to enter the box through a very little
hole. I suppose you know that bees were held
sacred to the Muses, and that there is in Greek
legend a symbolic relation between bees and
poetry.

If you want to know what kind of songs Comatas sang and what kind of life he represented,
you will find all this exquisitely told by Theocritus;
and there is a beautiful little translation in prose
of Theocritus, Bion and Moschus, made by An-
drew Lang, which should delight you to read.
Another day I shall give you examples of such
translations. Then you will see what true idyllic
poetry originally signified. These Greeks, although trained scholars and philosophers, understood not only that human nature in itself is a
beautiful thing, but also that the best way to study
human nature is to study the life of the peasants
and the common people. It is not to the rich and
leisurely, not to rank and society, that a poet must
go for inspiration. He will not find it there.
What is called society is a world in which nobody
is happy, and in which pure human nature is afraid

to show itself. Life among the higher classes in
all countries is formal, artificial, theatrical; poetry
is not there. Of course no kind of human community is perfectly happy, but it is among the
simple folk, the country folk, who do not know
much about evil and deceit, that the greater proportion of happiness can be found. Among the
youths of the country especially, combining the
charm of childhood with the strength of adult
maturity, the best possible subjects for fine pure
studies of human nature can be found. May I
not here express the hope that some young Japanese poet, some graduate of this very university,
will eventually attempt to do in Japan what Theocritus and Bion did in ancient Sicily? A great deal
of the very same kind of poetry exists in our own
rural districts, and parallels can be found in the
daily life of the Japanese peasants for everything
beautifully described in Theocritus. At all events
I am quite sure of one thing, that no great new literature can possibly arise in this country until
some scholarly minds discover that the real force
and truth and beauty and poetry of life is to be
found only in studies of the common people—not
in the life of the rich and the noble, not in the
shadowy life of books.

Well, our English poet felt with the Greek
idylists, and in the poem called "An Invocation"
he beautifully expresses this sympathy. All of us,
he says, should like to see and hear something of

the ancient past if it were possible. We should
like, some of us, to call back the vanished gods
and goddesses of the beautiful Greek world, or to
talk to the great souls of that world who had the
experience of life as men—to Socrates, for example, to Plato, to Phidias the sculptor, to Per-
icles the statesman. But, as a poet, my wish would
not be for the return of the old gods nor of the
old heroes so much as for the return to us of some
common men who lived in the Greek world. It is
Comatas, he says, that he would most like to see,
and to see in some English park—in the neigh-
bourhood of Cambridge University, or of Eton
College. And thus he addresses the spirit of
Comatas:

O dear divine Comatas, I would that thou and I
Beneath this broken sunlight this leisure day might lie;
Where trees from distant forests, whose names were
    strange to thee,
Should bend their amorous branches within thy reach
    to be,
And flowers thine Hellas knew not, which art hath made
    more fair,
Should shed their shining petals upon thy fragrant hair.

Then thou shouldst calmly listen with ever-changing looks
To songs of younger minstrels and plots of modern books,
And wonder at the daring of poets later born,
Whose thoughts are unto thy thoughts as noontide is to
    morn;

And little shouldst thou grudge them their greater
    strength of soul,
Thy partners in the torch-race, though nearer to the goal.

   .   .   .   .   .

Or in thy cedarn prison thou waitest for the bee:
Ah, leave that simple honey and take thy food from me.
My sun is stooping westward. Entrancèd dreamer, haste;
There's fruitage in my garden that I would have thee
    taste.
Now lift the lid a moment; now, Dorian shepherd, speak;
Two minds shall flow together, the English and the
    Greek.

A few phrases of these beautiful stanzas need
explanation. "Broken sunlight" refers, of course,
to the imperfect shade thrown by the trees under
which the poet is lying. The shadow is broken
by the light passing through leaves, or conversely,
the light is broken by the interposition of the
leaves. The reference to trees from distant forests no doubt intimates that the poet is in some
botanical garden, a private park, in which foreign
trees are carefully cultivated. The "torch race"
is a simile for the pursuit of knowledge and truth.
Greek thinkers compare the transmission of
knowledge from one generation to another, to the
passing of a lighted torch from hand to hand, as
in the case of messengers carrying signals or ath-
letes running a mighty race. As a runner runs
until he is tired, or until he reaches the next sta-
tion, and then passes the torch which he has been

carrying to another runner waiting to receive it,
so does each generation pass on its wisdom to the
succeeding generation, and disappear. "My sun
is stooping westward" is only a beautiful way of
saying, "I am becoming very old; be quick, so that
we may see each other before I die." And the
poet suggests that it is because of his age and his
experience and his wisdom that he could hope to
be of service to the dear divine Comatas. The
expression, "there is fruitage in my garden," refers to no material garden, but to the cultivated
mind of the scholar; he is only saying, "I have
strange knowledge that I should like to impart to
you." How delightful, indeed, it would be, could
some university scholar really converse with a living Greek of the old days!

There is another little Greek study of great and
simple beauty entitled "The Daughter of Cleo-
menes." It is only an historical incident, but it is
so related for the pleasure of suggesting a profound truth about the instinct of childhood. Long
ago, when the Persians were about to make an
attack upon the Greeks, there was an attempt to
buy off the Spartan resistance, and the messenger
to the Spartan general found him playing with
his little daughter, a child of six or seven. The
conference was carried on in whispers, and the
child could not hear what was being said; but she
broke up the whole plot by a single word. I shall
quote a few lines from the close of the poem,

which contain its moral lessons. The emissary
has tried to tempt him with promises of wealth
and power.

> He falters; for the waves he fears,
>   The roads he cannot measure;
> But rates full high the gleam of spears
>   And dreams of yellow treasure.
> He listens; he is yielding now;
>   Outspoke the fearless child:
> "Oh, Father, come away, lest thou
>   Be by this man beguiled."
> Her lowly judgment barred the plea,
>   So low, it could not reach her.
> *The man knows more of land and sea,*
>   *But she's the truer teacher.*

All the little girl could know about the matter
was instinctive; she only saw the cunning face of
the stranger, and felt sure that he was trying to
deceive her father for a bad purpose—so she
cried out, "Father, come away with me, or else
that man will deceive you." And she spoke
truth, as her father immediately recognized.

There are several more classical studies of extraordinary beauty; but your interest in them
would depend upon something more than interest
in Greek and Roman history, and we can not study
all the poems. So I prefer to go back to the
meditative lyrics, and to give a few splendid examples of these more personal compositions. The
following stanzas are from a poem whose Latin

title signifies that Love conquers death. In this
poem the author becomes the equal of Tennyson
as a master of language.

The plunging rocks, whose ravenous throats
  The sea in wrath and mockery fills,
The smoke that up the valley floats,
  The girlhood of the growing hills;

The thunderings from the miners' ledge,
  The wild assaults on nature's hoard,
The peak that stormward bares an edge
  Ground sharp in days when Titans warred;

Grim heights, by wandering clouds embraced
  Where lightning's ministers conspire,
Grey glens, with tarns and streamlet laced,
  Stark forgeries of primeval fire.

These scenes may gladden many a mind
  Awhile from homelier thoughts released,
And here my fellow men may find
  A Sabbath and a vision-feast.

I bless them in the good they feel;
  And yet I bless them with a sigh;
On me this grandeur stamps the seal
  Of tyrannous mortality.

The pitiless mountain stands so sure,
  The human breast so weakly heaves,
That brains decay while rocks endure,
  At this the insatiate spirit grieves.

But hither, oh ideal bride!
  For whom this heart in silence aches,
Love is unwearied as the tide,
  Love is perennial as the lakes.

Come thou. The spiky crags will seem
  One harvest of one heavenly year,
And fear of death, like childish dream,
  Will pass and flee, when thou art here.

Very possibly this charming meditation was
written on the Welsh coast; there is just such
scenery as the poem describes, and the grand peak
of Snowdon would well realize the imagination of
the line about the girlhood of the growing hills.
The melancholy of the latter part of the composition is the same melancholy to be found in
"Mimnermus in Church," the first of Cory's
poems which we read together. It is the Greek
teaching that there is nothing to console us for
the great doubt and mystery of existence except
unselfish affection. All through the book we find
the same philosophy, even in the beautiful studies
of student life and the memories of childhood. So
it is quite a melancholy book, though the sadness
be beautiful. I have given you examples of the
sadness of doubt and of the sadness of love; but
there is yet a third kind of sadness—the sadness
of a childless man, wishing that he could have a
child of his own. It is a very pretty thing, simply
entitled "Scheveningen Avenue"—probably the

name of the avenue where the incident occurred.
The poet does not tell us how it occurred, but we
can very well guess. He was riding in a street
car, probably, and a little girl next to him, while
sitting upon her nurse's lap, fell asleep, and as she
slept let her head fall upon his shoulder. This is
a very simple thing to make a poem about, but
what a poem it is!

> Oh, that the road were longer
>   A mile, or two, or three!
> So might the thought grow stronger
>   That flows from touch of thee.
>
> *Oh little slumbering maid,*
>   *If thou wert five years older,*
> *Thine head would not be laid*
>   *So simply on my shoulder!*
>
> *Oh, would that I were younger,*
>   *Oh, were I more like thee,*
> *I should not faintly hunger*
>   *For love that cannot be.*
>
> A girl might be caressed
>   Beside me freely sitting;
> A child on knee might rest,
>   And not like thee, unwitting.
>
> Such honour is thy mother's,
>   Who smileth on thy sleep,
> Or for the nurse who smothers
>   Thy cheek in kisses deep.

And but for parting day,
   And but for forest shady,
From me they'd take away
   The burden of their lady.

Ah thus to feel thee leaning
   Above the nursemaid's hand,
Is like a stranger's gleaning
   Where rich men own the land;

Chance gains, and humble thrift,
   With shyness much like thieving,
No notice with the gift,
   No thanks with the receiving.

Oh peasant, when thou starvest
   Outside the fair domain,
Imagine there's a harvest
   In every treasured grain.

Make with thy thoughts high cheer,
   Say grace for others dining,
And keep thy pittance clear
   From poison of repining.

There is an almost intolerable acuity of sadness in the last two mocking verses, but how pretty and how tender the whole thing is, and how gentle-hearted must have been the man who wrote it! The same tenderness reappears in references to children of a larger growth, the boys of his school. Sometimes he very much regrets the necessity of discipline, and advocates a wiser method of deal-

ing with the young. How very pretty is this little
verse about the boy he loves.

> Sweet eyes, that aim a level shaft,
>   At pleasure flying from afar,
> Sweet lips, just parted for a draught
>   Of Hebe's nectar, shall I mar
> By stress of disciplinal craft
>   The joys that in your freedom are?

But a little reflection further on in the same
poem reminds us how necessary the discipline must
be for the battle of life, inasmuch as each of those
charming boys will have to fight against evil—

> yet shall ye cope
> With worlding wrapped in silken lies,
> With pedant, hypocrite, and pope.

One might easily lecture about this little volume for many more days, so beautiful are the
things which fill it. But enough has been cited to
exemplify its unique value. If you reread these
quotations, I think you will find each time new
beauty in them. And the beauty is quite peculiar.
Such poetry could have been written only under
two conditions. The first is that the poet be a
consummate scholar. The second is that he must
have suffered, as only a great mind and heart could
suffer, from want of affection.

CHAPTER XV

THE other day when we were reading some of
the poems in "Ionica," I promised to speak in another short essay of Theocritus and his songs or
idyls of Greek peasant life, but in speaking of him
it will be well also to speak of others who equally
illustrate the fact that everywhere there is truth
and beauty for the mind that can see. I spoke
last week about what I thought the highest possible kind of literary art might become. But the
possible becoming is yet far away; and in speaking of some old Greek writers I want only to em-
phasize the fact that modern literary art as well
as ancient literary art produced their best results
from a close study of human nature.

Although Theocritus and others who wrote
idyls found their chief inspiration in the life of
the peasants, they sometimes also wrote about the
life of cities. Human nature may be studied in
the city as well as in the country, provided that a
man knows how to look for it. It is not in the
courts of princes nor the houses of nobles nor the
residences of the wealthy that such study can be
made. These superior classes have found it nec-

312

essary to show themselves to the world very cautiously; they live by rule, they conceal their emotions, they move theatrically. But the ordinary, everyday people of cities are very different; they speak their thoughts, they keep their hearts open, and they let us see, just as children do, the good or the evil side of their characters. So a good poet and a good observer can find in the life of cities subjects of study almost as easily as in the country. Theocritus has done this in his fifteenth idyl. This idyl is very famous, and it has been translated hundreds of times into various languages. Perhaps you may have seen one version of it which was made by Matthew Arnold. But I think that the version made by Lang is even better.

The scene is laid in Alexandria, probably some two thousand years ago, and the occasion is a religious holiday—a *matsuri*, as we call it in Japan. Two women have made an appointment to go together to the temple, to see the festival and to see the people. The poet begins his study by introducing us to the chamber of one of the women.

GORO. "Is Praxinoe at home?"

PRAXINOE. "Dear Gorgo, how long is it since you have been here! She is at home. The wonder is that you have got here at last! Eunoe, come and see that she has a chair and put a cushion on it!"

G. "It does most charmingly as it is."

P. "Do sit down."

How natural this is. There is nothing Greek about it any more than there is Japanese; it is simply human. It is something that happens in Tokyo every day, certainly in houses where there are chairs and where it is a custom to put a cushion on the chair for the visitor. But remember, this was two thousand years ago. Now listen to what the visitor has to say.

"I have scarcely got to you at all, Praxinoe! What a huge crowd, what hosts of carriages! Everywhere cavalry boots, everywhere men in uniform! And the road is endless; yes, you really live too far away!"

Praxinoe answers:

"It is all for that mad man of mine. Here he came to the ends of the earth and took a hall, not a house, and all that we might not be neighbours. The jealous wretch, always the same, ever for spite."

She is speaking half in jest, half in earnest; but she forgets that her little boy is present, and the visitor reminds her of the fact:

"Don't talk of your husband like that, my dear girl, before the little boy,—look how he is staring at you!—Never mind, Zaphyrion, sweet child, she is not speaking about papa."

P. "Our Lady! (Persephone) The child takes notice!"

Then the visitor to comfort the child says "Nice

papa," and the conversation proceeds. The two talk about their husbands, about their dresses, about the cost of things in the shops; but in order to see the festival Praxinoe must dress herself quickly, and woman, two thousand years ago, just as now, takes a long time to dress. Hear Praxinoe talking to her maid-servant while she hurries to get ready:

"Eunoe, bring the water and put it down in the middle of the room,—lazy creature that you are. Cat-like, always trying to sleep soft! Come, bustle, bring the water; quicker! I want water first,—and how she carries it! Give it me all the same;—don't pour out so much, you extravagant thing! Stupid girl! Why are you wetting my dress? There, stop, I have washed my hands as heaven would have it. Where is the key of the big chest? Bring it here."

This is life, natural and true; we can see those three together, the girlish young wife hurrying and scolding and chattering naturally and half childishly, the patient servant girl smiling at the hurry of her mistress, and the visitor looking at her friend's new dress, wondering how much it cost and presently asking her the price. At last all is ready. But the little boy sees his mother go out and he wants to go out too, though it has been decided not to take him, because the crowd is too rough and he might be hurt. Here the mother first explains, then speaks firmly:

"No, child, I don't mean to take you. Boo! Bogies! There is a horse that bites! Cry as much as you please, but I cannot have you maimed."

They go out, Praxinoe and Gorgo and the maid-servant Eunoe. The crowd is tremendous, and they find it very hard to advance. Sometimes there are horses in the way, sometimes wagons, occasionally a legion of cavalry. We know all this, because we hear the chatter of the women as they make their way through the press.

"Give me your hand, and you, Eunoe, catch hold of Eutychis,—for fear lest you get lost. . . . Here come the kings on horses! My dear man, don't trample on me. Eunoe, you fool-hardy girl, will you never keep out of the way? Oh! How tiresome, Gorgo, my muslin veil is torn in two already. . . . For heaven's sake, sir, if you ever wish to be fortunate, take care of my shawl!"

STRANGER. "I can hardly help myself, but for all that I will be as helpful as I can."

The strange man helps the women and children through the pushing crowd, and they thank him very prettily, praying that he may have good for-tune all his life. But not all the strangers who come in contact with them happen to be so kind. They come at last into that part of the temple ground where the image of Adonis is displayed; the beauty of the statue moves them, and they utter exclamations of delight. This does not please some of the male spectators, one of whom exclaims, "You tiresome women, do cease your endless cooing talk! They bore one to death with their eternal broad vowels!"

They are country women, and their critic is probably a purist—somebody who has studied Greek as it is pronounced and spoken in Athens. But the women bravely resent this interference with their rights.

GORGO. "Indeed! And where may this person come from? What is it to you if we are chatterboxes? Give orders to your own servants, sir. Do you pretend to command the ladies of Syracuse? If you must know, we are Corinthians by descent, like Bellerophon himself, and we speak Peloponnesian. Dorian women may lawfully speak Doric, I presume."

This is enough to silence the critic, but the other young woman also turns upon him, and we may suppose that he is glad to escape from their tongues. And then everybody becomes silent, for the religious services begin. The priestess, a comely girl, chants the psalm of Adonis, the beautiful old pagan hymn, more beautiful and more sensuous than anything uttered by the later religious poets of the West; and all listen in delighted stillness. As the hymn ends, Gorgo bursts out in exclamation of praise:

"Praxinoe! The woman is cleverer than we

fancied! Happy woman to know so much!—
Thrice happy to have so sweet a voice! Well,
all the same, it is time to be making for home;
Diocleides has not had his dinner, and the man is
all vinegar,—don't venture near him when he
is kept waiting for dinner. Farewell, beloved
Adonis—may you find us glad at your next
coming."

And with this natural mingling of the sentimen-
tal and the commonplace the little composition
ends. It is as though we were looking through
some window into the life of two thousand years
ago. Read the whole thing over to yourselves
when you have time to find the book in the library,
and see how true to human nature it is. There
is nothing in it except the wonderful hymn, which
does not belong to to-day as much as to the long
ago, to modern Tokyo as much as to ancient
Greece. That is what makes the immortality of
any literary production—not simply truth to the
life of one time, but truth to the life of every time
and place.

Not many years ago there was discovered a
book by Herodas, a Greek writer of about the
same period. It is called the "Mimes," a series
of little dramatic studies picturing the life of the
time. One of these is well worthy of rank with
the idyl of Theocritus above mentioned. It is the
study of a conversation between a young woman
and an old woman. The young woman has a

husband, who left her to join a military expedition and has not been heard of for several years. The old woman is a go-between, and she comes to see the young person on behalf of another young man, who admires her. But as soon as she states the nature of her errand, the young lady becomes very angry and feigns much virtuous indignation. There is a quarrel. Then the two become friends, and we know that the old woman's coming is likely to bring about the result desired. Now the wonder of this little study also is the play of emotion which it reveals. Such emotions are common to all ages of humanity; we feel the freshness of this reflection as we read, to such a degree that we cannot think of the matter as having happened long ago. Yet even the city in which these episodes took place has vanished from the face of the earth.

In the case of the studies of peasant life, there is also value of another kind. Here we have not only studies of human nature, but studies of particular social conditions. The quarrels of peasants, half good natured and nearly always happily ending; their account of their sorrows; their gossip about their work in the fields—all this might happen almost anywhere and at almost any time. But the song contest, the prize given for the best composition upon a chosen subject, this is particularly Greek, and has never perhaps existed outside of some place among the peasant folk. It was the poetical side of this Greek life of the peasants, as recorded by Theocritus, which so much influenced the literatures of the seventeenth and eighteenth centuries in France and in England. But neither in France nor in England has there ever really been, at any time, any life resembling that portrayed by Theocritus; to-day nothing appears to us more absurd than the eighteenth century habit of picturing the Greek shepherd life in English or French landscapes. What really may have existed among the shepherds of the antique world could not possibly exist in modern times. But how pretty it is! I think that the tenth idyl of Theocritus is perhaps the prettiest example of the whole series, thirty in number, which have been preserved for us. The plan is of the simplest. Two young peasants, respectively named Battus and Milon, meeting together in the field, talk about their sweethearts. One of them works lazily and is jeered by the other in consequence. The subject of the jeering acknowledges that he works badly because his mind is disturbed—he has fallen in love. Then the other expresses sympathy for him, and tells him that the best thing he can do to cheer himself up will be to make a song about the girl, and to sing it as he works. Then he makes a song, which has been the admiration of the world for twenty centuries and has been translated into almost every language possessing a literature.

"They all call thee a gipsy, gracious Bombyca, and lean, and sunburnt;—'tis only I that call thee honey-pale.

"Yea, and the violet is swart and swart the lettered hyacinth; but yet these flowers are chosen the first in garlands.

"The goat runs after cytisus, the wolf pursues the goat, the crane follows the plough,—but I am wild for love of thee.

"Would it were mine, all the wealth whereof Croesus was lord, as men tell! Then images of us, all in gold, should be dedicated to Aphrodite, thou with thy flute, and a rose, yea, or an apple, and I in fair attire and new shoon of Amyclae on both my feet.

"Ah, gracious Bombyca, thy feet are fashioned like carven ivory, thy voice is drowsy sweet, and thy ways—I can not tell of them."

Even through the disguise of an English prose translation, you will see how pretty and how simple this little song must have been in the Greek, and how very natural is the language of it. Our young peasant has fallen in love with the girl who is employed to play the flute for the reapers, as the peasants like to work to the sound of music. His comrades do not much admire Bombyca; one calls her "a long grasshopper of a girl"; another finds her too thin; a third calls her a gipsy, such a dark brown her skin has become by constant exposure to the summer sun. And the lover, looking at her, is obliged to acknowledge in his own mind that she is long and lean and dark and like a gipsy; but he finds beauty in all these characteristics, nevertheless. What if she is dark? The sweetest honey is darkish, like amber, and so are beautiful flowers, the best of all flowers, flowers given to Aphrodite; and the sacred hyacinth on whose leaves appear the letters of the word of lamentation "Ai! Ai!"—that is also dark like Bombyca. Her darkness is that of honey and flowers. What a charming apology! He cannot deny that she is long and lean, and he remains silent on these points, but here we must all sympathize with him. He shows good taste. It is the tall slender girl that is really the most beautiful and the most graceful, not the large-limbed, strong-bodied peasant type that his companions would prefer. Without knowing it, he has fallen in love like an artist. And he is not blind to the grace of slenderness and of form, though he cannot express it in artistic language. He can only compare the shape of the girl's feet to the ivory feet of the divinities in the temples—perhaps he is thinking of some ivory image of Aphrodite which he has seen. But how charming an image does he make to arise before us! Beautiful is the description of the girl's voice as " drowsy sweet." But the most exquisite thing in the whole song is the final despairing admission that he can not describe her at all—"and thy ways, I can not tell of them"! This is one of the most beautiful expressions in any poem ancient or modern, because of its supreme truth. What mortal ever could describe the charm of manner, voice, smile, address, in mere words? Such things are felt, they can not be described; and the peasant boy reaches the highest height of true lyrical poetry when he cries out "I can not tell of them." The great French critic Sainte-Beuve attempted to render this line as follows—"*Quant à ta manière, je ne puis la rendre!*" This is very good; and you can take your choice between it and any English translation. But good judges say that nothing in English or French equals the charm of the original.

You will find three different classes of idyls in Theocritus; the idyl which is a simple song of peasant life, a pure lyric expressing only a single emotion; the idyl which is a little story, usually a story about the gods or heroes; and lastly, the idyl which is presented in the form of a dialogue, or even of a conversation between three or four persons. All these forms of idyl, but especially the first and the third, were afterward beautifully imitated by the Roman poets; then very imperfectly imitated by modern poets. The imitation still goes on, but the very best English poets have never really been able to give us anything worthy of Theocritus himself.

However, this study of the Greek model has given some terms to English literature which every student ought to know. One of these terms is amœbæan,—amœbæan poetry being dialogue poetry composed in the form of question and reply. The original Greek signification was that of alternate speaking. Please do not forget the word. You may often find it in critical studies in essays upon contemporary literature; and when you see it again, remember Theocritus and the school of Greek poets who first introduced the charm of amœbæan poetry. I hope that this little lecture will interest some of you in Theocritus sufficiently to induce you to read him carefully through and through. But remember that you can not get the value of even a single poem of his at a single reading. We have become so much accustomed to conventional forms of literature that the simple art of poetry like this quite escapes us at first sight. We have to read it over and over again many times, and to think about it; then only we feel the wonderful charm.

INDEX

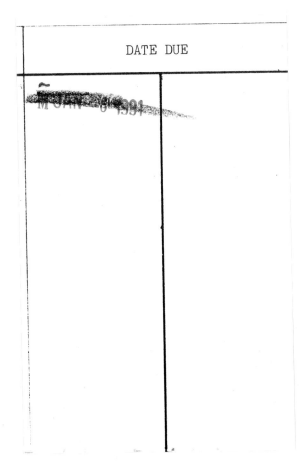